Productivity in the United States

Members of the Advisory Panel to
the Total Factor Productivity Project

John B. Boatwright
Exxon Corporation, U.S.A.

Malcolm Burnside
American Telephone & Telegraph
    Company

William Christopher
Management Counsel

Virginia Dwyer
American Telephone & Telegraph
    Company

John A. Gorman
Bureau of Economic Analysis
Department of Commerce

John Kraft
Division of Advanced Productivity
    Research and Technology
National Science Foundation

Jerome Mark
Bureau of Labor Statistics
Department of Labor

Geoffrey Moore
National Bureau of Economic
    Research

Harold C. Passer
Eastman Kodak Company

Edgar Weinberg
National Center for Productivity
    and Quality of Working Life

PRODUCTIVITY IN THE UNITED STATES

Trends and Cycles

John W. Kendrick
and Elliot S. Grossman

THE JOHNS HOPKINS UNIVERSITY PRESS
BALTIMORE AND LONDON

Manufactured in the United States of America

The Johns Hopkins University Press, Baltimore, Maryland 21218

The Johns Hopkins Press Ltd., London

Library of Congress Catalog Card Number 79-3678
ISBN 0-8018-2289-0

Library of Congress Cataloging in Publication data will be found on the last printed page of this book.

Contents

Tables

Illustrations

Foreword

Productivity has become a major issue of public policy in recent years, but only rarely is the discussion based on a thorough knowledge of the facts. This study, sponsored by The Conference Board under a grant from the National Science Foundation, presents a comprehensive set of estimates of productivity in the U.S. business economy by major sector and industry for the period 1948-76 with preliminary sector estimates for 1977 and 1978. Many of these are series that are not available elsewhere. In addition to the estimates of real product per hour of labor (produced by the Bureau of Labor Statistics), this study provides ratios of real product to capital and to total factor inputs—and on a quarterly as well as an annual basis.

The most important and most contentious issue is the retardation in the trend of productivity that has taken place since the mid-1960s. This is documented, and those industry groups in which retardation was most pronounced and those which continued to perform at or above their earlier trend-rates are identified. The economic effects of secular and cyclical movements in productivity are analyzed, with particular reference to costs, prices and production. The causes of productivity advance, and of the slow-down, are detailed both for the business economy as a whole and in terms of its major industry divisions. The analysis of causal forces is, of course, particularly important as background for consideration of policy options to promote the growth of productivity.

The project was originally planned and organized by John W. Kendrick, professor of economics at the George Washington University, whose earlier works on productivity for the Natural Bureau of Economic Research are landmarks in the field. When Dr. Kendrick left the project staff in the spring of 1976 to serve as Chief Economist of the U.S. Department of Commerce, direction of the project was taken over by Elliot S. Grossman. Upon Kendrick's return in April 1977, he and Grossman collaborated in completing the research and writing the report. Grossman was responsible for Chapters 3 and 6, the first part of Chapter 5, and for the summaries of these materials in Chapter 1; Kendrick wrote the remainder of the text. They were assisted throughout in the statistical work by Jean Lomask.

The authors also enjoyed the counsel of an Advisory Panel. The Panel met in September 1976 to review the research plan and early results, and again in May 1978 to discuss a preliminary draft of the report. The Conference Board is grateful to the Panel members for their extensive review of the project and their many helpful suggestions.

The Board arranged for publication of the report by the Johns Hopkins University Press. In view of the importance of the topic and of the estimates and analytical findings, we feel that the report should be readily available not only to the Associates of The Conference Board, but also to a wider audience.

Edgar R. Fiedler
Vice President for Economic Research
The Conference Board

Productivity in the United States

CHAPTER 1

Introduction and Summary

Introduction

The behavior of productivity during the recovery from the 1973-75 business contraction appears to confirm the fact that the trend rate of productivity growth since the mid-1960s has been significantly slower than during the prior two decades. This is true regardless of whether productivity is measured in terms of the familiar output per labor hour ratio, or the more inclusive total tangible factor productivity relationship, which takes account of capital as well as labor inputs. Following the initial upsurge of productivity in 1975-76, which is usual in the early stages of expansion, the rate of productivity advance has decelerated to the slower growth path of the previous decade.

Relatively poor productivity performance since 1966 has aggravated other economic problems in the United States. It has slowed the growth of real labor compensation per worker and of real income per capita. This, in turn, may have contributed to the acceleration of money wage-rate increases, while providing a lesser productivity offset to those increases, which has quickened the pace of price inflation. This has affected the international competitiveness of American goods, especially those produced by the industries in which the productivity slowdown and relative price increases have been greatest. Further, slowing growth has made more difficult the achievement of social goals, including adequate national security, on top of rising real personal incomes.

Clearly, the achievement of a higher productivity growth rate in the years ahead would help alleviate these problems. It is not the purpose of this study to develop specific policy recommendations for accelerating productivity. But it does provide a useful background for analysis of the current situation and outlook and for policy formulation in two main ways.

In the first place, this study provides a new body of annual and quarterly productivity statistics for the period since 1948 to supplement the official output per labor hour estimates. These statistics will be useful to analysts generally in tracking and analyzing productivity developments. Second, we have used the estimates to analyze some of the basic relationships between productivity and associated variables, both those that are causes of productivity change and those that reflect economic impact, particularly on unit costs, prices, and profits.

With respect to the new estimates, we build on the official series by developing time series of output per unit of capital input and per unit of combined labor and capital input. The latter multifactor productivity measures, usually called "total factor productivity" (TFP) are particularly important in revealing the net savings in real factor costs per unit of output achieved over time, and thus the increase in productive efficiency generally. Even for those who are primarily interested in labor productivity, the new estimates make possible the calculation of capital per unit of labor input, which is an important part of the explanation of changes in output per hour. The official estimates, prepared by the Bureau of Labor Statistics (BLS) in the U.S. Department of Labor, are confined to output per hour series. TFP estimates have been published by the National Bureau of Economic Research, but do not go beyond 1966 on an industry basis and 1969 for major sectors.[1] Following the basic procedure pioneered by the National Bureau, we have revised the estimates back to 1948 and extended them through 1976. Also, estimates have been developed for the first time of TFP on a quarterly basis for major sectors since 1948, for manufacturing industry groups since 1954, and for nonmanufacturing groups since 1965. The quarterly series are essential for cycle analysis. Whereas BLS publishes quarterly estimates of real product per hour for major sectors, our estimates supplement these by presenting output/capital ratios and TFP for the sectors, and in terms of thirty-one major industry groups.

In addition to developing productivity estimates to supplement the official series, we describe the basic trends and cyclical movements in the several productivity ratios and analyze their relationships with associated variables. In the analysis, we consider both causal factors underlying productivity changes and the economic impacts of the changes. In particular,

---

[1] See John W. Kendrick, *Postwar Productivity Trends in the United States, 1948-1969* (New York: National Bureau of Economic Research, 1973).

we examine the interrelationships among productivity, factor prices, unit costs, product prices, and profits, which lie at the heart of our private enterprise system. Important in analyzing the inflationary trends of our times, these interrelationships are also central to analysis of cyclical fluctuations in economic activity, as pointed out long ago by Wesley C. Mitchell and more recently documented by Geoffrey Moore with respect to the ratio of prices to unit costs.[2] Our analysis supplements this work by analyzing the relationships in terms of capital costs in relation to prices as well, thus explaining more fully the movements of unit profits. Also, by examining the cyclical timing of productivity change by industry group, we are able to identify those industries in which retardation of productivity change during expansion tends to decrease unit profits and thus foreshadow and contribute to the subsequent downturn in economic activity.

With respect to casual factors, the macroeconomic analysis relies largely on the "growth accounting" approach pioneered by Edward F. Denison.[3] By this approach, the various causal forces are specified and their relative contributions to the TFP growth rate are quantified. But this approach is importantly supplemented in the final chapter by relating differential rates of productivity change in the twenty manufacturing industries to differences in levels or in rates of change in causal factors.

The findings of this study with respect to productivity trends and cycles, their causes and economic impacts, will be of use to business as well as to the general public in understanding a key element in the broader economic environment within which companies operate. More specifically, those in business may find it of value to compare the productivity performance of their companies with that of the industries within which they are classified. There has been a significant increase in the number of companies with productivity measurement systems since The Conference Board published the first edition of its handbook on the subject in 1961.[4] Companies are also linking formal productivity improvement programs to their measurement efforts. After all, the individual producing unit is where the action is with respect to the cost-reducing innovations in the organization and technology of production, which is the chief long-run factor behind productivity advance.

---

[2] For specific references to the work of Mitchell and Moore, see Chapter 5 and the bibliography.

[3] Edward F. Denison, *Accounting for United States Economic Growth, 1948-1969* (Washington: The Brookings Institution, 1974).

[4] John W. Kendrick and Daniel Creamer, *Measuring Company Productivity: Handbook with Case Studies* (New York: The Conference Board, first edition 1961; second edition 1965).

We now present a summary of the study. Since it follows the chapter headings, it provides a preview of the scope and plan of the work, as well as highlighting its major findings.

Summary

Chapter 1. Introducton and Summary.   This chapter introduces the study by pointing out the importance of the growth of productivity, defined as output in relation to labor and other inputs. Productivity advance is the chief source of rising real labor compensation per worker and of increased planes of living generally; it is anti-inflationary by providing an offset to increasing wage rates and other input prices; and it helps enhance the international competitiveness of domestic production. The present study contributes to better understanding of productivity by, first of all, providing estimates of output per unit of capital and of TFP for the U.S. business economy by thirty-one major industry groups that importantly supplement the output per labor hour estimates prepared by the Bureau of Labor Statistics. Also, the full range of estimates has been developed on a quarterly basis since 1954 by manufacturing and since 1965 by nonmanufacturing industry, which further supplements the official output per hour estimates that are available only for four major sectors on a quarterly basis. In the second place, the estimates make possible a fuller analysis of trends and cycles in productivity and associated variables than is possible using labor productivity estimates alone. Most of the rest of this report is devoted to a discussion of findings.

Chapter 2. Productivity Concepts, Meaning, and Measurements.   The physical volume of output of a firm, industry, or economy depends on the quantities of labor and other inputs employed in production and on the productive efficiency of those inputs. Changes in productive efficiency can conveniently be calculated from ratios of output to the associated inputs. The basic measure in this study is the ratio of real product by industry (gross output less purchased materials and other "intermediate" products—a value-added measure) to the associated labor and capital factor inputs. Changes in this TFP ratio indicate the net savings achieved in use of the basic factors per unit of net output and thus the increase in productive efficiency.

We also use ratios of output (real product) to labor and capital inputs separately. These partial productivity ratios reflect changes in input mix (factor substitutions) as well as changes in productive efficiency. For example, the familiar output per labor hour ratio usually rises as a result of increased amounts of equipment and other capital goods per worker, as well as because of increased efficiency.

The meaning of changes in TFP is best understood in terms of a listing and rough quantification of the chief causal forces contributing to productivity growth. As shown below in Table 2-1, about half of overall productivity growth between 1948 and 1966 was due to advances in productive knowledge, as cost-reducing technological innovations were incorporated in the organization and instruments of production. A major part of the technological progress came from research and development programs. More than one-fifth of productivity growth was accounted for by each of two other causal factors: increases in the quality of labor, due primarily to increased education and training per worker; and to economies of scale, augmented by higher rates of utilization of capacity in 1966 than in 1948. More than 10 percent of productivity growth was contributed by resource reallocations, particularly the relative shift of labor from lower-pay to higher-pay industries. The net impact of government on business appears to have been about neutral, as increased services were offset by increased requirements and regulations. Declining average quality of natural resources and several other factors appear to have had a small negative impact.

Between 1966 and 1976, the rate of growth in total factor productivity slowed by half to a 1.4 percent average annual rate. Table 2-1 indicates that volume-related factors accounted for about half of the slowdown, reflecting primarily the incomplete recovery in 1976 from the 1974-75 recession. More basically, slower advances in applied knowledge accounted for about 20 percent of the deceleration. The other major negative factors were unfavorable changes in the labor force mix and in interindustry resource reallocations. Declining quality of natural resources and increased government regulation also had larger negative impacts than in the earlier period.

With respect to the sources of the estimates, the annual output series are the sector and industry real product estimates of the U.S. Department of Commerce, interpolated quarterly by other series for the industry groups. The labor hour estimates are also based largely on official sources, primarily the Department of Labor. The capital series are based on Conference Board estimates published in *The National Wealth of the United States, by Major Sector and Industry* (1976), as subsequently revised and extended. The labor and capital input indexes were combined on the basis of the proportions of the two factors in gross national income by sector and industry. These proportions differ considerably among industries, but the labor proportion has generally risen.

Chapter 3. Long-Term Trends in Total Factor Productivity. Between 1948 and 1976, real output as measured for the U.S. private domestic business economy expanded at a 3.5 percent annual average rate. Over this same period, labor input increased at a 0.5 percent rate and real gross capital 2.4 percent. Total factor input, a weighted average of labor and capital inputs, rose at an average rate of 1.2 percent. Thus, total factor productivity—the gain in output above the growth in labor and capital inputs—grew at a 2.3 percent rate. Total factor productivity of the three major sectors that comprise the private domestic business economy rose at varying rates during the postwar period: farming, 3 percent; manufacturing, 2.1 percent; and nonfarm-nonmanufacturing, 2 percent.

Labor productivity, which is the measure of productivity published by the Bureau of Labor Statistics, U.S. Department of Labor, rose at a 3 percent rate for the private domestic business economy between 1948 and 1976 and for the three major sectors: farming, 5 percent; manufacturing, 2.7 percent; and nonfarm-nonmanufacturing, 2.4 percent. The capital-labor ratio, which gives an indication of the rate of substitution of capital for labor, rose at a 1.9 percent rate for the private domestic business economy, and at 5.2, 2.3, and 1.3 percent rates for the farming, manufacturing, and nonfarm-nonmanufacturing sectors, respectively.

The variation in growth rates in total and partial factor productivity among industries is much greater than that exhibited by the major sectors. The largest rate of increase in TFP since 1948 has been in the communications industry, 4.2 percent. Within the manufacturing sector the electrical machinery industry has the strongest rise in TFP at 3.7 percent, and the primary metals industry had the least rise, only 0.1 percent.

Rates of change in TFP over time also vary greatly and are influenced by differences in the intensity of economic activity, labor and capital utilization, and other such factors that are related to the business cycle. Measured by cycle peak-to-peak years, subperiod growth rates of private domestic business economy productivity varied from a high of 3.4 percent between 1960 and 1966, to a low of 1.5 percent between 1966 and 1969. The major sectors and industries also exhibited similar variation in their rates of productivity change.

Since the mid-1960s, there appears to have been a slowdown in total and partial factor productivity. Between 1948 and 1966 TFP of the private domestic business economy grew at a 2.9 percent rate, slowing to 1.4 percent between 1966 and 1976. The three major sectors also exhibited slowdowns in their productivity growth rates, as did twenty-eight of the thirty-one industries.

The private domestic business economy, as well as the nonfarm-non-manufacturing sector, had statistically significant declines in their TFP trend rates of growth after 1966, based on regression analysis of their productivity trends. The other two sectors, manufacturing and farming, showed no statistically significant decline in their productivity trends. Within the manufacturing sector, eight industries exhibited statistically significant declines in their productivity growth rates. For example, the productivity trend for the lumber industry declined 3.5 percentage points after 1966, dropping from a 3.9 percent rate prior to 1966 to 0.4 percent thereafter. In contrast, two industries, apparel and paper, exhibited significant increases in their productivity rates of growth after 1966.

Chapter 4. Productivity, Costs, and Prices. In the first section of this chapter, we look at the anti-inflationary role of productivity in the large nonfinancial corporate sector of the economy. Factor costs account for about 90 percent of gross product originating in the sector, so changes in factor costs per unit of output (real product) are the chief component of changes in average prices, as measured by the implicit price deflator for gross product. The other element is indirect business taxes (less subsidies) per unit, which rose more than unit factor costs prior to 1966 and thus augmented price inflation.

Changes in unit factor costs are approximately equal to changes in factor prices *less* changes in the corresponding productivity ratios (all changes expressed as percentage rates). Between 1948 and 1976, the 2.2 percent average annual rate of increase in TFP offset more than 40 percent of the 5.2 percent rate of increase in average factor prices. As a result, unit factor costs rose by 2.9 percent and the price deflator by 3 percent a year, on average. During the subperiod 1948-66, TFP increases offset about two-thirds of the more moderate increases in factor prices. But between 1966 and 1976, the lower rates of increase in TFP offset only one-fifth of the accelerated increases in wage rates and other factor prices. The separate contributions of unit labor costs and of unit capital costs are shown in the tables. Despite the larger increases in output per labor hour than in the output/capital ratio, unit labor cost increases accounted for about two-thirds of the price rise, less prior to 1966 and somewhat more thereafter. Increases in unit fixed capital costs (depreciation and interest) also contributed significantly to inflation, particularly after 1966. But unit profits were a moderating influence, especially between 1966 and 1976 when rates of return on investment and net worth dropped sharply.

On an industry basis, rates of change in productivity were negatively correlated with the rates of change in unit factor costs and product prices.

This is to be expected, since relative changes in factor prices as a whole are not tied into relative changes in productivity on an industry basis. Because higher productivity growth has meant lower increases (or declines) in product prices, there is a significant positive correlation between relative industry changes in productivity and in output. The relationship is reciprocal because of economies of scale. Production increases are generally strong enough to offset the labor-saving impact of productivity change in progressive industries, and employment of the factors rose almost as much in the high productivity growth industries as in the less progressive ones. The tables make it possible to trace through the interrelationships for each of the thirty industry groups, but we do so for only two at either end of the productivity growth spectrum in order to illustrate concretely the general relationships.

The relationships are less pronounced for the partial productivity ratios and associated labor and capital prices, unit costs, and inputs. It also appears that the relationships are weaker than they were before World War II, reflecting structural changes in the U.S. economy.

Chapter 5. Cyclical Behavior of Productivity and Related Variables.   During expansionary periods, as measured from cyclical troughs to peaks, output and total factor productivity of the major sectors exhibit stronger growth than over the full twenty-eight year period. One reason is the movement from low rates of capital utilization back toward more efficient utilization rates. Examination of the postwar expansion periods does not indicate any pattern toward slower or faster productivity growth. Total factor productivity growth rates also vary quite considerably among the manufacturing industries, ranging from 0.6 percent to 6.5 percent for the nonelectrical machinery and chemical industries, respectively. The high correlation between output and productivity rates of change is apparent when comparing the median rates of change for the industries.

In contrast, the performance of productivity and output over contraction periods—measured from cyclical peaks to troughs—is poor. The weak showing of productivity during such periods is due to output falling faster than labor and capital inputs. Compared to the other two sectors, the brunt of the postwar recessions was borne by the manufacturing sector, which had a median rate of decline of output of 10.8 percent. Further, the median decline in manufacturing productivity was 3.2 percent. Those industries that exhibited large declines in output also tended to have stronger declines in their productivity during periods of economic contraction. Cyclically sensitive industries were the most severely affected. The transportation industry, for example, had a median rate of decline in its output of over 30 percent and a 22 percent decline in its productivity.

Analysis of our quarterly estimates for the nonfinancial corporate sector confirms and supplements the explanation of cyclical fluctuations developed by Wesley C. Mitchell. With respect to the labor variables, the quarterly estimates indicate that rates of change in output per hour peak many quarters before the upper turning point of the typical cycle, and lead by 1 quarter at the trough, on average. In conjunction with the behavior of average hourly earnings, the labor productivity changes result in unit labor costs rising faster than prices for at least 6 quarters before the reference cycle peak, reducing unit profits for 5 quarters before, which contributes importantly to the downturn. Conversely, the acceleration of changes in output per hour prior to the trough, while average hourly compensation is still decelerating, causes a drop in unit labor cost and an increase in the price/cost ratio, widening profit margins and setting the stage for the subsequent recovery.

Our new estimates of capital productivity and cost, and of total factor productivity and average factor price, make possible an extension of the Mitchell approach. Thus, we find that rates of change in output per unit of capital reach a peak 5 quarters before the reference cycle turning point, on average. In conjunction with the behavior of the price of capital, this is associated with a downturn in the ratio of price to unit capital cost prior to the peak, which reinforces the profit squeeze associated with the behavior of labor costs. At the trough, however, changes in the ratio of price to unit capital costs are coincident. Because of the predominance of labor costs in total unit costs, however, the ratio of price to total unit cost shows the same leads at both the peak and the trough as does the ratio of price to unit labor cost alone.

Chapter 6. Causal Analysis of Productivity Change within Manufacturing Industries.   The causes of TFP growth within the twenty manufacturing industries are examined, using regression analysis. Specifically, the rates of change in productivity are regressed against a number of variables including: capacity utilization, education, research and development expenditures, hours worked per week, degree of concentration within the industry, degree of unionization, percent of man-days idled due to work stoppages, composition of work force by sex, type of worker, and age, layoff and quit rates, and shifts of employment among industries.

The ability of the regression analysis to sort out the important causes of the variation in TFP was hampered by the high intercorrelation among the explanatory variables. Among the several possible equations, the set of variables having the best relationship to productivity are degree of unionization (negative), rate of change in the degree of unionization (positive), research and development spending as a percent of gross product originating (positive), degree of concentration (positive), variation in rate of capacity utilization (negative), and women as a percentage of all employees (positive). Eighty-six percent of the variation in TFP among the manufacturing industries is explained by these six variables.

A similar analysis was used to examine the post-1966 slowdown in productivity. First, the 1948-66 and, separately, the 1966-76 productivity growth rates were regressed on the six variables used in the 1948-76 analysis. Of the six variables, only research and development (R&D) spending had a significant and stable relationship with productivity over the two subperiods. This suggests that the causes of the *slowdown* are to be found in variables other than those used in the regressions, with the important exception of investment in R&D.

CHAPTER 2

Productivity Concepts, Meaning, and Measurements

There is a whole family of productivity concepts and measures, ranging from ratios of output to individual classes of inputs, such as the familiar output-per-hour measure, to multifactor or total productivity measures relating output to all associated inputs in real terms. In this chapter, we explain the leading productivity concepts, and discuss the meaning of each. This involves reference to the main causes of productivity growth, which provides a background for further analysis of causal factors in a later chapter. Since the interpretation of the productivity ratios also depends on the method used in measuring the physical volumes of outputs and inputs, we summarize the methodology and sources for our estimates.

The Productivity Concept and Its Meaning

The concept of productivity is rooted in the notion of the "production function." Simply stated, the production function merely expresses the fact that the physical volume of output depends on the physical volume of resource inputs used in the production process, and on the efficiency with which they are used, i.e., on their productivity. The productivity variable is best gotten at as a ratio of output to input. It is, of course, influenced by many forces that we shall be discussing in this and subsequent chapters.

The notion and underlying reality of the production function applies to the smallest producing units of firms, and to successively larger aggregations of producing units ranging from four-digit industries—according to the Standard Industrial Classifications by which industries are defined primarily in terms of product groupings—up through the ten broadest one-digit industry groups. Industries may be further grouped in broader sectors, such as primary (extractive), secondary (commodity producing) and tertiary (service) industries, as well as combined for the entire business economy. In principle, production and productivity may also be measured for the nonbusiness sectors—households, private nonprofit institutions, and general governments. Because of the inadequacies of output data for the latter sectors, which comprise only about 15 percent of the domestic economy according to the official GNP estimates, we confine the measures of productivity in this study to the business economy and its major industry groupings—twenty manufacturing and ten nonfarm-nonmanufacturing groups, and farming.

The broadest productivity measure is one that relates gross output to all associated inputs—the services of the basic factors of production: labor, and capital goods, including land and other natural resources; and intermediate products comprising materials, supplies, energy, and other purchased services. But when all the industries of the economy are consolidated, the interindustry sales and purchases of intermediate products cancel out, and the resulting net output, or real final product, is seen to result from a combination of the basic factor services of labor and capital, including land, or real factor cost. The official gross national product estimates of the U.S. Department of Commerce are calculated on the nonduplicative, value-added basis, by industry.

We follow the concepts and methodology developed at the National Bureau of Economic Research[1] and estimate total tangible factor productivity (TFP) by relating real product to the real factor costs in the business economy, by industry group. This has the advantage that TFP for the business sector is a weighted average of TFP in the component industries. For some purposes, it is better to relate measures of gross output to all inputs, factors plus intermediate products. Such total productivity measures directly show the saving achieved in intermediate inputs, including energy, as well as in factor services per unit of input. They are particularly useful for company information systems, since managements continually strive to employ a least-cost combination of all cost elements—purchased items as well as the services of resident factors. But even if one wished to calculate the broader measures, sometimes called "multi-factor productivity," adequate data on intermediate

---

[1] See John W. Kendrick, *Productivity Trends in the United States*, and *Postwar Productivity Trends in the United States, 1948-1969* (New York: National Bureau of Economic Research, 1961 and 1973). More detailed discussions of concept and methodology than given here are contained in the first two chapters of each of the Bureau volumes.

inputs are not readily available for at least half the business sector. In any case, the TFP measures for industry groups have the virtue of consistency with the measures for the entire business economy.

There are several ways to calculate TFP, including econometric techniques that provide estimates of the trend-rate of productivity growth. The simplest method, yielding the most flexible measures, is to calculate ratios of real product to real factor costs in successive periods and then to convert the ratios to index numbers. In this study we use a 1967 base (=100.0) for the index numbers, although the weights used to combine outputs are based on 1972 unit values. The ratios make possible calculations of period-to-period percent changes (annual or quarterly rates compounded to give annual rates), as well as calculations of average annual percentage rates of change. Although the latter can be obtained from trend-lines fitted to the time-series, we generally compute them by the compound interest formula between peak years of the business cycle for consistency with rates of change in the component output and input series. The earliest and most recent peak years of the period covered by this study are 1948 and 1973, spanning a quarter-century. Estimates back to the latter nineteenth century are available from the NBER monographs referred to earlier.[2]

Only when output is related to all associated inputs, as in the TFP measures, can one estimate the net savings in real costs per unit of input, and thus increases in productive efficiency. Although output per hour is the most common form of productivity ratio, it is affected by substitution of capital for labor, as well as by changes in productive efficiency. In the next section, we explore in some depth the meaning of changes in productive efficiency; suffice it to say here that the chief cause of a rising long-run trend in TFP is cost-reducing technological progress.

In addition to the TFP measures, ratios of output to each of the categories of inputs for which separate data exist may be calculated. Index numbers of such ratios are called "partial productivity" measures. They reflect changes in input-mix resulting from factor substitutions, as well as technological advance and other forces impinging on productive efficiency. In this study, we present estimates of only the two major partial productivity ratios: output per unit of labor input (hours), and output per unit of capital input. These ratios are useful in showing savings achieved over time in each major class of input per unit of output (more clearly indicated when the ratios are inverted). They do *not* indicate the productivity of the individual factor, nor productive efficiency generally, since factor substitutions are involved.

---

[2] See footnote 1. The present study revises the NBER estimates for the years 1948-69 based on subsequent data, extends the series through 1976, and adds quarterly interpolations.

The substitutions occur because of changes in relative factor prices and in the composition of output, as well as because of the nature of technological changes. In general, capital has grown faster than labor in the U.S. economy and in practically all industries, which is associated with the fact that the price of labor (compensation per hour) has generally risen significantly more than the price of capital (capital goods prices as well as the interest rate in the case of debt-financed capital, and the profit rate in the case of equity-financed capital). Finally, it should be noted that the TFP ratios are, in effect, a weighted average of the two major partial productivity ratios, or of as many ratios of output to various types of labor and capital inputs as it is possible and desirable to compute. Of interest in their own right, the partial productivity ratios are also an important ingredient, together with factor prices, in explaining changes in labor and capital costs per unit of output, as is done in Chapter 4.

We have stated that total tangible factor productivity ratios indicate the economies in use of real factor costs per unit of real product achieved over time, and thus the increase in the efficiency with which factor inputs are used in production. Another way of stating it is that changes in TFP reflect the net effect of all factors that contribute to production other than changes in the quantities of the basic factors of production employed by the producing unit, industry, or sector. Sometimes productivity change is referred to as "the residual," since the rate of change in TFP is the same as the difference between the rate of change in real product and a weighted average of the rates of change in the tangible factor inputs. Some years ago, the tangible factor productivity residual was also challengingly called a "measure of our ignorance" concerning the sources of economic growth over and above the growth of the labor and capital inputs. Since we measure inputs without allowance for changes in the quality of the labor and capital, such quality improvements are obviously one important cause of productivity improvement. But there are other factors that we shall now summarize. A clear understanding of the meaning of productivity change in terms of major determinants is important for developing quantitative models designed to explain the causes of productivity growth, as in Chapter 6, and as background for formulation of policies to promote economic progress.

Causal Forces

The meaning of changes (or differences) in productivity ratios or residuals becomes much clearer when the causal forces are explicitly set forth and, if possible, quantified. Although the causal factors can explain differences in *levels* of productivity between the same industries or sectors in different countries, or between producing units in the same industry (whether domestic or foreign), for the sake of expositional simplicity in this section we refer to causes of productivity *change*. Also, in order to make the discussion more concrete, we refer to estimates of the contributions of each of the causal factors to the growth of total factor productivity in the U.S. business economy between 1948 and 1966, based largely on the estimates of Edward Denison,[3] supplemented by some additional estimates described in a recent paper by Kendrick.[4] We use the period 1948-66 since it precedes the productivity slowdown of the past decade, documented in the next chapter. We also employ the analytical framework developed here in order to help explain the causes of the retardation of productivity advance in the 1966-76 decade. For this decade, most of the estimates were made by Kendrick, since Denison has not yet published a full set of his estimated components of growth after 1969.

Basic Values and Institutions.   The estimates contained in Table 2-1 below, around which the following discussion centers, relate to *proximate* determinants of productivity change in terms of seven major categories. It should be kept in mind that underlying the more immediate determinants are the *basic* values and institutions of a society, which change much more slowly. The relevant values, or attitudes, are those relating to the desire for material advancement, the willingness to work hard and to save and invest for the future, the willingness to assume responsibilities and risks, to innovate, and to adapt to change. Some observers claim that the work ethic and the drive for higher real incomes have weakened in the United States during the past decade. But it would be difficult to document this based on the actions of most individuals and significant social groups.

The institutional framework of the economy in the United States has to do with the laws and regulations governing the private enterprise sector, both the competitive and the regulated utility sectors, and the institutional forms and practices that have evolved in both the private and public sectors. This is obviously a complex subject that we can not do justice to here. In general, changes in both values and institutions would affect productivity change mainly through their effects on investment and the other proximate determinants, which are themselves interrelated. In our later cross-industry analysis

[3] See Edward F. Denison, *Accounting for United States Economic Growth 1948-1969* (Washington: The Brookings Institution, 1974).

[4] See John W. Kendrick, "Total Investment and Productivity Developments," paper presented to a joint session of the American Economic and Finance Associations, New York, December 30, 1977.

Table 2-1. U.S. domestic business economy, sources of growth of real gross product, contributions to growth in percentage points, 1948-66 and 1966-76

	1948-66	1966-76
Real gross product	3.9	2.8
Tangible factor inputs	1.0	1.4
Total factor productivity	2.9	1.4
Advances in knowledge	1.4	1.1
Formal R&D	.85	.7
Informal	.3	.3
Changes in rate of diffusion	.25	.1
Changes in quality of labor	.6	.5
Education and training	.6	.8
Health and vitality	.1	.1
Age-sex composition	−.1	−.4
Actual/potential efficiency	−	−
Changes in quality of land	−	−.1
Resource reallocations	.3	.1
Self-employment to employment	.1	−
Interindustry labor shifts	.4	.1
Weighting effects	−.2	−
Volume-related factors	.6	−.2
Economies of scale	.5	.3
Intensity of demand	.1	−.5
Irregular factors	−	−
Net government impact	−	−.1
Government services to business	.1	.1
Business services to government	−.1	−.2
Residual factors, n.e.c.	−	.1

Source: John W. Kendrick, "Total Investment and Productivity Developments," paper prepared for a joint session of the American Economic and Finance Associations, New York, December 30, 1977 (available on request to the author), based for the 1948-66 period mainly on estimates from Edward F. Denison, *Accounting for United States Economic Growth, 1948-1969* (Washington, D.C.: The Brookings Institution, 1974).

of causal factors in Chapter 6, we do include several variables that relate specifically to institutional arrangements, such as the degree of industry concentration and the percentage of employees in various industries belonging to labor unions.

Advances in Productive Knowledge.   The most important determinant of productivity growth is what Denison calls "advances in knowledge"—technological and organizational—as applied in production. It results from cost-reducing innovations in the ways and means of production. Even the invention and commercial development of new and improved consumer goods, another aspect of technological progress, indirectly contribute to productivity advance, since real unit cost reductions are usually greatest in the early stages of production of new goods. So a steady stream of new products helps maintain the growth of productivity and real product through the "learning-curve" effect, and an increasing (decreasing) volume of new products would accelerate (decelerate) productivity growth.

Denison estimates that roughly 1.4 percentage points, about half of our 2.9 percent estimate of the average annual rate of increase in TFP in the business sector 1948-66, is attributable to advances in productive knowledge. In this century, technological progress has come increasingly from organized research and development (R&D) programs. Ever since the industrial laboratory became a high-growth industry after World War I, until the mid-1960s, R&D has been the fountainhead of new producers goods and processes, application of which has been a major source of technological advance. Based on his estimates of the growth of real stocks resulting from outlays for R&D,[5] Kendrick has estimated that more than half of the advances in knowledge in 1948-66 has come from this source. But after 1966, there was a distinct slowing in the growth of real stocks of productive knowledge resulting from R&D outlays, which dropped from 3 percent of GNP in 1966 to 2.2 percent in 1976. As a result, the contribution of formal R&D programs to advances in knowledge declined from 0.85 percentage point in the earlier subperiod to 0.70 in the subsequent decade.

Advances in knowledge are also affected by the rate of diffusion of new technology. Since cost-reducing technology is embodied in new producers' goods, changes in the average age of business fixed capital is one indicator of changes in the rate of diffusion. Between 1948 and 1966, Commerce Department estimates of the real business stocks of structures and equipment show a decline in their average age of more than three years. This suggests an acceleration in the rate of diffusion of new technology of around 0.25 percentage point a year over the eighteen-year period. Between 1966 and 1976, h wever, average age declined only about one year, contributing 0.1 percentage point to the rate of technological progress.

The residual 0.3 percentage point, or over 20 percent of the contribution of advances in knowledge 1948-66, is attributable to informal inventive and innovative activity. One would expect this source of progress to continue to be significant, since many small improvements in new processes and producers goods are made by managers and workers generally as they apply and adapt new technology in the production process. And the activities of "lone wolf" inventors, which are not covered by the R&D statistics, continue to be important, although no longer the chief source of technological

[5] See John W. Kendrick, *The Formation and Stocks of Total Capital* (New York: National Bureau of Economic Research, 1976).

progress as in the nineteenth century. There is no independent indicator of informal inventive and innovative activity. But even assuming it continued after 1966 at the same pace as during the 1948-66 subperiod, it is evident that the total contribution of advances in applied knowledge slowed from 1.4 to 1.1 percentage points in 1966-76, due to the declining contributions of the other two elements just reviewed (see Table 2-1).

Changes in the Quality of Labor.   Denison includes changes in labor quality in his estimates of labor input. Since we measure labor input in terms of hours worked without adjustment for changes in the productive capacity of workers, we treat the several variables affecting labor quality as part of the explanation of changes in total factor productivity as measured here.

The most important of these variables is the increase in the average education of persons engaged in production. Based on earnings differentials of persons with differing attained levels of formal education (standardizing for differences in ability), Denison estimated the contribution of education to productivity growth in 1948-66 at about 0.5 percentage point. Kendrick obtained a 0.6 percentage point contribution based on the rate of growth of the real stock of knowledge resulting from outlays on education and training, and the rate of return on these intangible investments. Since Denison's estimate did not include the effects of training programs, which absorb about one-sixth of the funds devoted to both education and training, the two estimates are consistent. For the decade 1966-76, Kendrick estimates that the stock of knowledge resulting from education and training grew even faster than in the prior subperiod, contributing 0.8 percentage point to growth.

With respect to health and vitality, which obviously influence worker efficiency, Denison estimates a 0.05 percentage point contribution from the reduction in the length of the workweek between 1948 and 1966. Kendrick estimates a like contribution from the growth of the real stocks resulting from investments in health and safety of the work-force. Together, these factors contribute a 0.1 percentage point to productivity growth in 1948-66, and a like amount in the subsequent decade.

Changes in the age-sex composition of the employed labor force also affect productivity, due to the differences in average hourly earnings of various age-sex groups, which are related at least in part to experience, or "learning by doing." Based on the effects of shifts among ten age-sex groups, Denison estimated a -0.1 percentage point effect of this factor in 1948-66, as the proportions of youth and women in the labor force rose—although not nearly as rapidly as in the following decade. Kendrick estimates the impact at -0.4 percentage point in the 1966-76 subperiod. By the 1980s, this factor will have a positive effect as the labor force matures.

Changes in the degree of effort expended by workers, which affects the ratio of actual to potential efficiency under given technology, can have a potentially significant effect on productivity. Unfortunately, there is no good way to measure it in the aggregate, although "work measurement" systems attempt to do so for selected groups of workers within companies or other organizations. Denison does not consider this to have been a significant variable over the period 1948-66, although there is a widespread opinion that labor efficiency may have declined somewhat after 1966, due to a weakening of the work ethic. Denison also notes that the actual allocation of workers among jobs relative to an optimum allocation affects productivity, but this variable is also not readily susceptible to measurement.

Changes in Quality of Land.   Economists have long enunciated the tendency toward diminishing returns in extractive industries as the average quality of land and other natural resources declines with increasing use beyond some point. In the past, this tendency has not been very pronounced in the United States due to discovery and development of new resource reserves, and it has been far more than offset by technological advances in agricultural and mineral industries, whose productivity gains were well above average prior to 1966. Since the extractive industries comprise less than 10 percent of GNP, it is our judgment that this factor contributed less than −.05 percent prior to 1966. We include it in the table, however, since there is evidence that the average quality of natural resources has declined faster in recent years, contributing about −0.1 percent in the 1966-76 decade. It may decline even more in the future, as the nation strives for greater energy independence.

It might seem logical to include changes in the average quality of capital goods, in addition to changes in the quality of labor and land. But that would be duplicative, since it is already covered by advances in knowledge as applied to the organization and instruments of production. Professor Dale Jorgenson estimates a variable he calls "the quality of capital," which reflects relative shifts in the use of capital among industries with differing rates of return. This variable we would classify under resource reallocations, discussed next, although it is changes in labor-mix that have had a more pronounced effect.

Resource Reallocations.   Resource allocation has to do with economic efficiency, i.e., production in conformity with the community's preferences. Optimum allocation is attained when all units of the same resource receive the same rate of remuneration equal to the value of its marginal product in all uses. Dynamic forces, particularly technological change, are continually causing resource reallocations. One aspect of efficiency is the speed with which resources move to higher productivity and more remunerative uses.

With respect to labor, Denison distinguishes two types of shifts that he perceives as increasing productivity—from farming into nonfarm industries, and from nonfarm self-employment into employee status. The latter shift he estimates to have contributed 0.1 percentage point between 1948 and 1966, although it appears to have had a negligible effect in the following decade. The former he estimates to have contributed 0.3 percentage point. To the latter we have added a 0.1 point based on our estimate of the effect of relative labor shifts among the thirty nonfarm industries for which we have estimates. So the table shows a 0.4 percentage point effect on all interindustry shifts in 1948-66. The effects of the farm-nonfarm shift played out in the following decade, and the 0.1 percentage point shown in Table 2-1, reflect chiefly the continuing shifts of labor among nonfarm industries.

Another effect of interindustry resource shifts is on the implicit relative weights accorded to industry productivity estimates. Thus, the declining relative weights of extractive industries, which had above average productivity advance prior to 1966, and the increasing relative weights of service industries with below average productivity advance, had a negative impact, partially offsetting the positive effects of resource reallocations between 1948 and 1966. Our computations using TFP estimates for the thirty-one industry groups, including farming, indicate a −0.2 percent impact over the eighteen-year period. But the impact was negligible during the 1966-76 decade.

Volume-Related Factors.   Next, there are several factors related to the rate and variability of economic growth. The first is the economies of scale that come with the growth of local, national, and international markets, permitting greater specializations of personnel, equipment, plants, and firms, and the spreading of overhead costs over increasing quantities of output. Denison estimates that scale economies account for around 10 percent of the growth rate. Thus, between 1948 and 1966, this factor contributed 0.5 percentage point, and 0.3 percentage point between 1966 and 1976.

Changes in rates of utilization of capacity, primarily a cyclical factor, can also affect growth rates if the utilization ratios differ significantly for the years between which the growth rates are calculated. Denison estimates that the ratio of actual to potential real gross business product was higher in 1966 than in 1948, contributing a 0.1 percentage point to the growth of productivity. But in 1976, the ratio of actual to potential was significantly below that in 1966, based on the estimates of the Council of Economic Advisers. The difference contributed −0.5 percentage point to the growth rate over the decade. The structure of demand in relation to that of supply capacities would also have some bearing, but is more difficult to quantify.

Also, the variability of demand affects productivity growth, but this operates mainly through the various types of investment associated with other causal factors already discussed.

Finally, there are various irregular, erratic forces, such as the weather and strikes, that affect short-run changes in production and productivity, but not the longer-run trends, as a rule.

Net Government Services to Business.   When dealing with the business sector alone, one must take account of the contributions of government to business productivity and, conversely, the impact on business unit costs of government reporting requirements, regulations, and so on. Kendrick calculates that increased government services to business in the form of infrastructure as well as direct services contributed a 0.1 percentage point to productivity growth in 1948-66; but that this was approximately offset by increased reporting and other requirements imposed on business by government. The positive contribution of government was the same during the decade after 1966 as before, but the negative impact of government requirements increased. Denison estimates that the average annual increase in unit real costs imposed by environmental and occupational health and safety regulations alone amounted to 0.2 percentage point.[6]

Residual Factors (Not Elsewhere Classified).   The last category is a residual, reflecting the net effect of variables not elsewhere classified, as well as the net effect of possible errors in the other estimates. A major residual factor is changes in those aspects of the legal, institutional, and social environment within which business operates that impact unit real costs. One example is the honesty of the public in general, and of customers, employees, and suppliers in particular, which affects costs via security outlays and losses from crime. In addition, n.e.c. includes various forces that are not reflected at all, or only partially, in the specified variables. Examples cited by Denison are changes in competitive or other pressures on enterprises to reduce costs, and changes in the average quality of managements not reflected in the labor quality variable. Another factor that was not significant in the 1948-66 period, but became so later, is changes in the relative prices of exports and imports, which affect the domestic factor resource cost of imports.

Obviously, more research is needed to improve the estimates of the impacts of the various causal forces on productivity growth. But the available

[6] See Edward F. Denison, "Effect of Selected Changes in the Institutional and Human Environment upon Output per Unit of Input," U.S. Department of Commerce, *Survey of Current Business* (January 1978): 21-44.

estimates cited in this review at least indicate the relative orders of magnitude during the post-1948 period. They also indicate the chief causes of productivity slowdown between the 1948-66 and 1966-76 subperiods. To recapitulate, volume-related factors—particularly the lower intensity of demand in 1976 compared with 1966—accounted for about half of the 1.5 percentage point deceleration in TFP growth. Slower advances in applied knowledge accounted for about 20 percent of the slowdown. The other major negative factors were changes in the labor-force mix and a less favorable impact of interindustry resource shifts. Declining quality of natural resources and increased government regulation also had more negative direct impacts. The one positive factor was an even faster increase in the average quality of labor, due to rising levels of education and training. But apparently the slowing of technological advance and of aggregate demand did not permit the full exploitation of this favorable development in terms of increased economic efficiency.

Summary of Sources and Methods

Output Measures.   The output numerators of our productivity ratios are estimates of real gross product originating in the business sector of the U.S. domestic economy, by major industry divisions, prepared by the Bureau of Economic Analysis (BEA), in the U.S. Department of Commerce.[7] For the manufacturing industry groups and several nonmanufacturing industries, comprising about half of the business economy, the current dollar estimates were converted by BEA to constant 1972 prices by the "double-deflation" method. That is, the value of gross production of each industry was deflated by index numbers of prices received, and the costs of intermediate product purchases were deflated by indexes of prices paid. The price series were largely drawn from the BLS wholesale price indexes. Real intermediate costs were then subtracted from the real gross production estimates in order to arrive at real gross product, which is a value-added measure as explained earlier. Although net of intermediate products, it is gross of capital consumption allowances.

For the other industry groups, for which adequate estimates of intermediate product purchases were lacking, two main alternative approaches were used. For industries in which intermediate purchases are minor, mainly

---

[7]See The National Income and Product Accounts of the United States, 1929-74, Statistical Tables, and the July 1977 *Survey of Current Business*, published by the Bureau of Economic Analysis, U.S. Department of Commerce.

in the service sector, gross product in current prices (as built up from factor costs and other charges) was deflated directly by prices received. For the other industries, base period gross product was extrapolated in other years by gross production measures, on the assumption that the ratio of value-added (gross product) to the value of gross production was relatively constant.

Despite the complexity of the deflation procedures, real gross business product obtained as the sum of real product originating in the component industries was very close in all years to gross business product obtained by the alternative procedure of deflating the final sales of the business sector by types of goods and services. Table 2-2 shows the relative size of the various sectors and the industry divisions of the business sector with which we are concerned for the base year 1972.

BEA also publishes quarterly estimates of real business product, broken down by farm, nonfarm, manufacturing, and nonmanufacturing groupings. In order to make possible a more detailed analysis of cylical movements of productivity and related variables, we have interpolated quarterly the BEA annual estimates of real product in the twenty manufacturing industry groups back to 1954 and the ten other nonfarm groups back to 1965, using various quarterly gross production measures. The statistical technique employed has been described in a report published by The Conference Board.[8]

For the manufacturing groups, mining, and electric and gas utilities, we used the corresponding components of the monthly Federal Reserve Board's index of industrial production as interpolators. For contract construction, we used quarterly estimates of the constant dollar volume of new construction put in place; for railroad and other transportation, revenue ton-miles of freight and passenger-miles or passengers of the various types of common carriers, weighted by revenue proportions in 1972; for communications, deflated revenues of telephone and telegraph companies; for trade, deflated retail sales and sales of merchant wholesalers; for finance and insurance, deposit turnover, the real value of new insurance written, and the volume of sales of stocks and bonds on the New York Stock Exchange, weighted by the relative contributions to national income in 1972; for real estate, the real stocks of tenant-occupied residential and rental nonresidential real estate (see below); and services were interpolated by the residual real gross product obtained by subtracting the quarterly estimates of the other nonfarm-non-manufacturing industry groups from the BEA total. Since the real product of services is a residual, the quarterly as well as the annual estimates of real

[8]John W. Kendrick, *The National Wealth of the United States by Major Sector and Industry*. The Conference Board, Report No. 698, 1976.

Table 2-2. *Gross national product by sector and industry, 1972*
(billions of dollars and percentage distribution)

	Billions of dollars	Percentage distribution	
		GNP by sector	Business sector by industry
Gross national product	1171.1	100.0	
Rest of world	7.0	0.6	
Gross domestic product	1164.1	99.4	
Government	137.4	11.7	
Federal	50.1	4.3	
State and local	87.3	7.5	
Households and institutions	37.2	3.2	
Households	5.3	0.5	
Private nonprofit institutions	31.9	2.7	
Business	989.5	84.5	100.0
Farm	33.7		3.4
Nonfarm	955.8		96.6
Manufacturing	288.8		29.2
Food	27.6		2.8
Tobacco	4.2		0.4
Textiles	9.3		0.9
Apparel	9.9		1.0
Lumber	8.9		0.9
Furniture	4.8		0.5
Paper	11.0		1.1
Printing and publishing	14.6		1.5
Chemicals	21.5		2.2
Petroleum	7.6		0.8
Rubber	9.0		0.9
Leather	2.1		0.2
Stone, clay, and glass	9.9		1.0
Other durables	148.4		15.0
Nonmanufacturing	667.0		67.4
Mining	18.9		1.9
Contract construction	56.6		5.7
Transportation	46.2		4.7
Railroad	10.3		1.1
Other	35.9		3.6
Communications	29.4		3.0
Electric, gas, and other utilities	28.0		2.8
Trade	201.2		20.3
Finance and insurance	43.7		4.4
Real estate	124.9		12.6
Services	97.3		9.8
Agricultural services, etc.	3.3		0.3
Government enterprises	17.5		1.8

product by industry add up to the BEA total for the business economy, exclusive of the two small groups of government enterprise, and forestry, fisheries, and agricultural services, which we do not include in the industry analysis.

Obviously, the quality of the quarterly output estimates is not as good as that of the annual. But since the quarterly numbers are tied into the annual estimates, they cannot develop any systematic bias. Even the annual real product estimates of BEA are themselves of varying quality. In general, the estimates for the commodity-producing industries and regulated groups (communications, utilities, and transportation) are better than those for the finance and service industry groups. In finance, the ouput estimates are essentially measures of labor input; hence, they tend to have a downward bias to the extent that productivity actually increased.

Input Measures. The Bureau of Labor Statistics (BLS) publishes quarterly annual estimates of hours of all persons engaged in production in the business economy, broken down by the farm, nonfarm, manufacturing, and non-farm-nonmanufacturing sectors. The estimates are published in conjunction with their quarterly releases on productivity (output per hour) in these sectors. We use the BLS hours estimates for the three sectors, and as the control totals for hours estimates for the manufacturing and nonmanu-facturing industry groups for which the Bureau does not publish compre-hensive hours data nor productivity estimates. Since the BLS also uses the BEA real product estimates as the numerator of their output per hour series, our sector estimates are virtually the same as theirs. In addition, we show the further industry breakdown, and also calculate output per unit of capital input (see below) and the combined TFP measures, which we believe im-portantly supplement the official series.

The BLS hours estimates comprise hours of employees, proprietors, and unpaid family workers. In order to distribute the manufacturing and nonmanufacturing totals by the component industry groups, we used the published BLS series on employment and average hours of production or nonsupervisory workers applied to all employees, and unpublished data on numbers of and average hours worked by proprietors and unpaid family workers, by industry groups. Since the latter unpublished series are available on an industry basis only from 1962 forward from labor force surveys, we used the employee distributions by industry in earlier years and quarters to distribute the proprietor and unpaid family worker totals. Ideally, we would have preferred the hours estimates to relate to hours worked rather than paid for. But the BLS estimates are actually a mixture of the two. Since time paid for but not worked has risen significantly since 1948, the BLS estimates, and therefore our industry estimates, rise somewhat faster than would a pure hours-worked series.

Labor input for each industry group and each sector is simply total hours without any internal weighting by occupational category within industries, or by industries within broader groups or sectors. In this, we depart from the primary National Bureau of Economic Research (NBER) procedure, by which industry hours were weighted by average hourly labor compensation to obtain labor input for broader groupings. Since labor has gradually shifted toward occupations and industries with higher pay, a weighted-hours series generally rises faster than unweighted hours. Such shift effects show up in our labor productivity estimates, rather than in labor input.

The capital inputs were assumed to move proportionally to real gross stocks of tangible capital—structures, land, equipment, and inventories—in each sector and industry group. Some estimators allow for some deterioration in the output-producing capacity of fixed capital goods as they age, but we do not consider it to be substantial, assuming adequate maintenance. The sources and methods used for estimating the real stocks of capital were described in *The National Wealth of the United States, by Major Sector and Industry*,[9] and need not be repeated here. It must be noted, however, that the earlier estimates, which went through 1975, were in terms of 1958 dollars; they have now been converted to a 1972 price base. The estimates for the manufacturing industry groups have been somewhat revised,[10] and the quarterly interpolations of the industry stock estimates were extended back to 1954.

The assumption that real gross capital stocks and inputs move proportionately is based on the notion that capital involves a real cost, regardless of rates of utilization. Some investigators prefer to adjust capital estimates for capacity utilization rates, which can be done from available estimates for manufacturing. Without the adjustment, changes in rates of utilization of capacity affect the productivity ratios rather than the input estimates.

Index numbers of labor and of capital inputs were combined into total input indexes, required for the TFP estimates, by the share of each factor in gross national income originating in each of the various industry groups and sectors. To reflect the gradually changing shares of labor and capital, we used 1948 weights for the period 1948-59; 1959 weights for 1959-69; 1969 weights for 1969-73; and 1973 weights for the subsequent years and quarters. The indexes were linked back from 1973 to avoid any discontinuities and converted to a 1972 comparison base. The labor percentage weights are shown in Table 2-3; the capital weights are 100 percent minus the labor weights.

[9] Ibid.

[10] Estimates of manufacturing capital by industry were made available by Daniel Creamer of The Conference Board.

Table 2-3. Relative weights of labor: shares of gross income originating*
in U.S. business economy by major industry groups (percentages)

	1948	1959	1969	1973
Business economy	63.9	64.3	65.1	68.8
Farming	56.4	59.7	49.1	31.8
Manufacturing	70.9	73.2	74.7	75.6
Food	68.8	72.3	75.1	78.1
Tobacco	50.1	39.8	39.1	41.2
Textiles	68.6	78.4	76.7	86.4
Apparel	86.1	90.7	88.5	90.5
Lumber	74.6	77.3	68.2	63.2
Furniture	86.7	87.8	83.3	91.7
Paper	63.3	67.1	70.5	68.8
Printing and publishing	82.3	82.9	79.4	80.6
Chemicals	53.9	55.0	61.4	61.0
Petroleum	27.1	40.1	35.0	30.2
Rubber	77.0	74.8	78.1	80.9
Leather	80.7	90.5	86.9	86.4
Stone, clay and glass	73.3	66.6	74.0	75.8
Primary metals	70.0	70.0	75.4	78.3
Fabricated metals	77.4	81.6	81.4	82.5
Machinery, except electrical	77.7	76.5	78.0	77.9
Electrical machinery	80.7	79.6	81.3	80.4
Transportation equipment	72.6	75.0	74.9	76.2
Instruments	80.4	74.0	68.6	76.3
Miscellaneous manufactures	77.2	78.1	82.7	80.7
Nonfarm-nonmanufacturing	62.3	59.8	60.8	68.4
Mining	57.2	55.8	59.2	59.6
Contract construction	92.6	94.7	92.1	93.2
Total transportation	79.7	81.0	80.0	82.3
Railroad	77.3	79.2	77.7	83.4
Nonrail	82.4	81.6	80.7	81.6
Communications	73.9	54.5	52.4	55.9
Public utilities	50.4	38.7	38.7	40.5
Trade	78.9	84.9	84.3	84.6
Finance and insurance	81.7	78.9	83.8	96.5
Real estate	11.5	7.4	7.4	8.0
Services	86.9	72.0	81.9	80.7

*Based on U.S. Department of Commerce estimates, after allocating net proprietors' income between compensation of labor and of property.

The index numbers for total input, and for labor and capital inputs separately, were then divided into index numbers of real gross product in order to yield the indexes of TFP and the partial-productivity ratios by sector and industry. Since the industry output and input measures are all consistent with the business sector totals, the productivity indexes for the business sector are, in effect, weighted averages of the indexes for the component industry groups. All indexes are contained in the Statistical Appendix.

CHAPTER 3

Long-Term Trends in
Total Factor Productivity

Estimates of productivity over broad spans of time give perspective to the ebb
and flow of gains in economic growth, real wages, and pressures on inflation.
Between 1948 and 1976, real product (output) as measured for the private
domestic business economy grew at a 3.5 percent rate.[1] Over the same post-
World War II period, labor input grew at a 0.5 percent rate, and capital 2.4
percent, or a weighted average increase in factor input of 1.2. Thus, total
factor productivity (TFP)—the gain in output above the growth in factor inputs—grew at a 2.3 percent rate.

Figure 3-1 shows the postwar trend in TFP of the private domestic business economy, as well as the more common labor productivity measure, output per labor hour, as published by the Bureau of Labor Statistics, U.S. Department of Labor, and the ratio of output to capital input. Even though
productivity has increased almost without interruption since 1948, the trend
has not been consistent, as evidenced by Table 3-1, which presents the rate
of growth of productivity for selected subperiods. Peak years (except for

[1] As measured by the compound interest formula. Even though this estimate is
more sensitive to the choice of the end-points, it has the advantage that the components
of the changes being measured add up to the total change. The choice of 1976 as an end-
point is somewhat unfortunate in that, unlike 1948, it is not a cycle peak. However,
1976 was used in this study, since it is the latest year available for analysis, and the use
of 1973 as an end-point does not lead to substantially different results (the 1948-73
rate of change in the private domestic business economy output is 3.8 percent). For further discussion on this point see, John W. Kendrick, *Postwar Productivity Trends in the
United States, 1948-1969* (New York: National Bureau of Economic Research, 1973),
pp. 36-37.

Table 3-1. Private domestic business economy: total factor productivity,
1948-76 and selected subperiods
(average annual percentage rates of growth)

Period	Rate of growth*		Period	Rate of growth
1948-53	3.4%		1966-69	1.5%
1953-57	2.1		1969-73	1.8
1957-60	2.1		1973-76	0.7
1960-66	3.4		1948-73	2.5
		1948-76 2.3%		
		1948-66 2.9		
		1966-76 1.4		

*Compound annual rate of change; years selected represent peak years (except 1976) that minimize impact of capital underutilization on the estimate of TFP.

Sources: U.S. Department of Commerce; U.S. Department of Labor; The Conference Board.

1976) have been chosen for the subperiods so as to minimize the impact of underutilization of capital that occurs during economic slowdowns. Over the entire 1948-76 period, productivity grew at a 2.3 percent rate. However, within this twenty-eight year period, productivity rates of change varied considerably, from a rate as high as 3.4 percent between 1960 and 1966—the longest period of uninterrupted economic growth since 1948—to 0.7 percent between 1973 and 1976. The last subperiod, of course, covers the worst postwar recession and less than two full years of recovery.

Although the increase in TFP was 1.3 percent between 1976 and 1977, preliminary estimates for 1978 indicate an increase of less than 0.5 percent. So even if the last subperiod were extended from 1973-76 to 1973-78, the average annual percentage change would be raised only from 0.7 to 0.8 percent, and the longer-period trends are unaffected. Since our industry estimates are available only through 1976, we are constrained to use the shorter span of years in describing recent developments. This should be kept in mind mainly in interpreting the industry rates of change that are differentially affected by cyclical forces.

Also it is evident in Figure 3-1 that in the late 1960s there appears a slowdown in productivity. Between 1948 and 1966 productivity grew at a 2.9 percent rate, but the rate dropped to 1.4 percent between 1966 and 1976. This slowdown is especially evident in the output-capital ratio. This ratio dropped over two-thirds of its 1948-66 rate of 1.5 percent to a small 0.3 percent rate after 1966. A combination of factors contributing to this post-1966 slowdown in the output-capital ratio is discussed below. What is apparent is that economic growth over the post-1966 period has been hampered by a slowdown (1966-67) and two full-fledged recessions, 1969-70 and 1973-75. Further, there appears to be a strong positive relationship between pro-

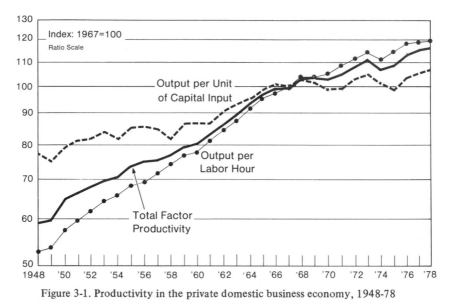

Figure 3-1. Productivity in the private domestic business economy, 1948-78

Sources: U.S. Department of Labor; U.S. Department of Commerce; Conference Board.

ductivity rates and rates of change in output. Thus, it is difficult to pinpoint the specific cause of changes in productivity rates of growth.

Though there are no directly comparable measures of total factor productivity available before 1948, Kendrick has previously reported[2] that the rate of change in TFP for the private domestic economy (which, unlike the private domestic business economy, includes the household sector) grew at a 1.3 percent rate between 1889 and 1919, then accelerated to 1.8 percent between 1919 and 1948, and to 2.5 percent from 1948 to 1966.[3] This great surge in productivity advances since 1889 does not reflect the pattern of acceleration-deceleration-acceleration in real growth. Between 1889 and 1919, real output of the private domestic economy increased at a 3.9 percent rate, then slowed to a 2.8 percent rate in the 1919 to 1948 period that included the Great Depression, and, after World War II, jumped back to a 4 percent rate through 1966.[4]

[2]Ibid., p. 41, Table 3-2.

[3]The estimate of TFP for 1948-66 is 2.9 percent. There are several differences between these two estimates, both in terms of methodology and in definition, the main differences being the exclusion of the government sector. Estimates of productivity growth within the government sector are problematical due to lack of direct measures of output and, therefore, usually lead to low estimates. Thus, including this sector would lower the overall rate of change in productivity.

[4]Kendrick, *Postwar Productivity Trends*, p. 41, Table 3-2. The rate of growth of output for private domestic business economy has been estimated here to be 3.9 percent, just slightly below the estimate for the private domestic economy.

The wavelike movement of economic growth came as a result of under-lying surges in inputs and/or productivity. The high rate of advance in output in the 1889-1919 period reflected a 2.6 percent rate of increase in labor and capital inputs. In contrast, from 1919 to 1948, a period that included the Great Depression, total factor inputs slowed to a 1 percent rate that was only partially offset by an acceleration in the rate of productivity change to a 1.8 percent rate from the 1.3 rate of the earlier period. Finally, during the post-war period, inputs increased at a rate of 1.5 percent, still considerably below the 1889-1919 experience, but this was augmented by an acceleration in total factor productivity to 2.5 percent. Thus, we see economic growth may be achieved by increases in labor and capital inputs, or by gains in the effi-ciency with which the inputs are utilized. As population growth rates and labor inputs decline, or level off, productivity gains become a more critical issue in our efforts to experience greater gains in output.

As mentioned earlier (Chapter 2) gains in productivity contribute to eco-nomic well-being by allowing increases in wages that need not be translated into higher prices (see Chapter 4 for a further discussion of the components of price changes) and, of equal importance, in increases in real output *per person*. Even though output grew at the same rate in the 1889-1919 period as in the 1948-66 period, most of the growth in the earlier period is due to increases in labor (as well as capital) per capita. In the postwar period, most of the high growth in real output is traceable to productivity gains that allow concomitant advances in per capita output. Between 1889 and 1948, real output measured by net national product per capita grew at a 2 percent rate, as it did from 1948 through 1976. Given all the problems in using real output per person as a measure of economic welfare or well-being, there is no question that society has advanced, materially at least, much faster in this century than during any period before in modern history, and much of this gain is due to the advances in productivity. The question becomes, then, can this favorable rate of productivity that has been experienced over the past three decades be continued in the future. This chapter describes the rates of change in productivity since 1948, how these rates differ among sectors and industries, and examines the slowdown in productivity since the mid-1960s.[5]

Sector Trends in Total Factor Productivity

Table 3-2 presents the trends in TFP as well as its components for the overall private domestic business economy and its major sectors: farm, nonfarm-

[5]The Council of Economic Advisers, in the 1977 *Economic Report of the Presi-dent* (Washington, D.C.: U.S. Government Printing Office, 1977), pp. 45-48, discusses the post-1966 slowdown in productivity and some of the likely causes.

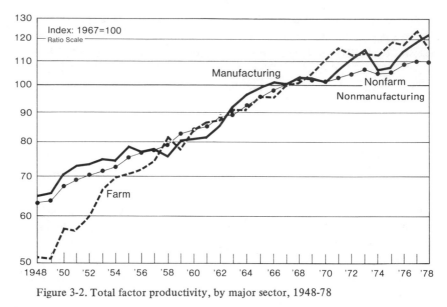

Figure 3-2. Total factor productivity, by major sector, 1948-78

Sources: U.S. Department of Labor; U.S. Department of Commerce; Conference Board.

nonmanufacturing, and manufacturing, as well as the nonfinancial business sector. Of course, the change in productivity for the private domestic business economy is a weighted average of the changes in productivity of the three major sectors, which, in turn, reflect the productivity growth among their component industries (Fig. 3-2).

During the postwar period (1948-76), real output of the private domestic business economy grew at a 3.5 percent annual rate. The growth rate among its component sectors ranged from 3.8 percent for the nonfarm-nonmanufacturing sector, to 3.3 percent for manufacturing, and 0.9 percent in the farm sector. The nonfinancial corporate business sector, which excludes most farms and other noncorporate enterprises, as well as financial (service) activities, grew at a relatively high rate of 4.2 percent.

Variation in productivity rates among sectors is associated with differing rates of growth of inputs. The nonfarm-nonmanufacturing and manufacturing sectors had increases in total factor inputs of 1.8 and 1.2 percent, respectively, which translate into rates of growth of TFP of 2 and 2.1 percent. In contrast, total factor input into the farm sector declined at a 2.1 percent annual rate, which reflects the 3.9 percent rate of decrease in labor input and a 1.1 percent increase in capital. Thus, farm productivity growth was 3 percent, almost half again as large as for the other two sectors.

The farm sector, however, is a small and declining contributor to total output and continues to play a lesser role in TFP of the overall economy. Yet, it must be mentioned that the farm sector's decline in labor input demonstrates the shift from rural to urban (and suburban) life, plus a tremendous rate of substitution of capital for labor (5.2 percent), way above that of the other two sectors. Of course, it is the introduction of new technology that has freed much of the rural population from farm work. This trend, however, has slowed, as shown by the subperiod growth rates for labor input, which has dropped from -4.5 percent between 1948 and 1966 to -2.9 percent thereafter.

The rates of growth of the partial productivity ratios also differ among the sectors. The output-labor ratio grew at a 3.0 annual rate for the private domestic business economy over the postwar period. The farm sector's 5 percent rise in labor productivity mirrors its decline in labor input. Within the manufacturing sector the output-labor ratio rose at a 2.7 percent rate, slightly faster than the 2.4 percent rate exhibited by the nonfarm-nonmanufacturing sector. The output-capital partial productivity ratio shows a different picture among the sectors. Overall, this ratio rose at a 1.1 percent rate for the private domestic business economy, which reflects the 0.2 percent average decline in the farm sector and increases of 1.1 and 0.3 percent for the nonfarm-nonmanufacturing and manufacturing sectors, respectively.

Rates of growth in the ratio of capital to labor do give some indication of the rates of substitution of capital for labor. This ratio also helps to explain the difference in growth rates of the two partial productivity ratios, and between them and TFP. For example, the rate of growth of TFP for the private domestic business economy of 2.3 percent is, in effect, a weighted average of the two productivity ratios, output-labor (3 percent) and output-capital (1.1 percent). The difference in the growth rates of the two partial productivity ratios equals the growth in the capital-labor ratio, 1.9 percent. Further, multiplying this difference of 1.9 percent by the base-period factor shares (labor 68.8, and capital 31.2, in 1973), 1.3 percent and 0.6 percent are obtained, which are approximately the differences between the rates of growth of TFP and of each of the partial productivity ratios.

Among the two nonfarm sectors, the manufacturing rate of capital-labor substitution of 2.3 percent was almost twice that of the nonfarm-nonmanufacturing sectors rate of 1.3 percent. Yet, the TFP rate for manufacturing is only 0.1 percentage point above that of the nonfarm-nonmanufacturing sector (2.1 and 2 percent, respectively), which indicates that not all advances in productivity are due to gains in capital relative to labor (so-

Table 3-2. *Trends of outputs, inputs, and productivity for major sectors (percent changes at annual rates)*

Output

	1948-76	1948-66	1966-76
Private domestic business economy	3.5	3.9	2.8
Nonfinancial corporate business	4.2	4.8	3.2
Farm	0.9	0.6	1.5
Nonfarm-nonmanufacturing	3.8	4.1	3.3
Manufacturing	3.3	4.2	1.8

Capital input

	1948-76	1948-66	1966-76
Private domestic business economy	2.4	2.4	2.5
Nonfinancial corporate business	3.3	3.4	3.2
Farm	1.1	1.2	0.9
Nonfarm-nonmanufacturing	2.6	2.5	2.8
Manufacturing	3.0	3.1	2.8

Labor input

	1948-76	1948-66	1966-76
Private domestic business economy	0.5	0.4	0.8
Nonfinancial corporate business	1.5	1.6	1.4
Farm	-3.9	-4.5	-2.9
Nonfarm-nonmanufacturing	1.3	1.0	1.8
Manufacturing	0.6	1.2	-0.4

Total factor input

	1948-76	1948-66	1966-76
Private domestic business economy	1.2	1.0	1.4
Nonfinancial corporate business	2.0	2.1	1.9
Farm	-2.1	-2.8	-0.7
Nonfarm-nonmanufacturing	1.8	1.6	2.2
Manufacturing	1.2	1.6	0.5

Total factor productivity

	1948-76	1948-66	1966-76
Private domestic business economy	2.3	2.9	1.4
Nonfinancial corporate business	2.2	2.7	1.3
Farm	3.0	3.5	2.2
Non-nonmanufacturing	2.0	2.5	1.1
Manufacturing	2.1	2.5	1.4

Output/labor ratio

	1948-76	1948-66	1966-76
Private domestic business economy	3.0	3.5	1.9
Nonfinancial corporate business	2.6	3.1	1.8
Farm	5.0	5.3	4.5
Non-nonmanufacturing	2.4	3.0	1.4
Manufacturing	2.7	2.9	2.2

Output/capital ratio

	1948-76	1948-66	1966-76
Private domestic business economy	1.1	1.5	0.3
Nonfinancial corporate business	0.9	1.4	0.0
Farm	-0.2	-0.6	0.6
Nonfarm-nonmanufacturing	1.1	1.5	0.5
Manufacturing	0.3	1.0	-0.9

Capital/labor ratio

	1948-76	1948-66	1966-76
Private domestic business economy	1.9	2.0	1.7
Nonfinancial corporate business	1.7	1.7	1.8
Farm	5.2	6.0	3.9
Nonfarm-nonmanufacturing	1.3	1.5	0.9
Manufacturing	2.3	1.9	3.1

Table 3-3. Total factor productivity by major sector, selected subperiods 1948-78
(average annual percentage rates of change)

Period	Farm	Nonfarm-nonmanufacturing	Manufacturing
1948-53	5.4%	2.5%	2.9%
1953-57	2.7	2.1	1.0
1957-60	3.8	2.2	1.1
1960-66	2.3	2.8	3.9
1966-69	3.2	1.3	0.9
1969-73	2.3	1.1	2.7
1973-76	1.1	0.8	0.1
(1973-78)^P	0.4	0.6	1.1
1948-76	3.0	2.0	2.1

P=preliminary
Sources: U.S. Department of Commerce; U.S. Department of Labor; The Conference Board.

called "embodied" advances), but are due to other factors not directly attributable to capital (or "disembodied" advances).

In addition to variations in productivity across sectors (and industries), there are also variations across time. Table 3-3 contains the subperiod peak-to-peak rates of change of productivity by major sector. Both the nonfarm-nonmanufacturing and the manufacturing sectors exhibit their highest growth in productivity during the 1960-66 period, and slowest gains between 1973 and 1976. The farm sector, on the other hand, achieved its highest gain in productivity between 1948 and 1953 and has exhibited a slowing trend of productivity growth since then. All three sectors exhibit considerable slowdown in their productivity changes since 1966. When the estimates are extended from 1976 to 1978, the relative performance of manufacturing is improved, but the rates of increase of the other two sectors are reduced.

Nonfarm-Nonmanufacturing Industries

The variability in growth rates of output, input and productivity ratios among one- and two-digit SIC (Standard Industrial Code) nonfarm-nonmanufacturing industries is shown by Table 3-4. Postwar (1948-76) average annual rates of growth in real output range from a high of 7.1 percent in the communications industry to a low of 1.7 percent for mining.

Within transportation, however, output of the railroad industry declined at a 0.7 percent rate, compared to a 3.4 percent average increase in nonrailroad transportation over the past three decades. Both capital and labor inputs into the railroad industry have declined since 1948, yet there has been

Table 3-4. Trends of outputs, inputs, and productivity for nonfarm-nonmanufacturing industries (percent changes at annual rates)

	Output			Capital input		
	1948-76	1948-66	1966-76	1948-76	1948-66	1966-76
Mining	1.7	2.1	1.1	0.7	0.3	1.5
Contract construction	2.6	4.5	-0.8	5.0	6.4	2.5
Total transportation	2.1	2.3	1.8	0.7	1.1	0.0
Railroad	-0.7	0.5	-2.8	-0.1	0.2	-0.7
Nonrail	3.4	3.4	3.4	4.1	5.3	1.9
Communications	7.1	6.7	7.8	5.8	5.6	6.0
Public utilities	5.8	7.2	3.3	4.3	4.1	4.7
Trade	3.8	4.0	3.4	3.4	3.8	2.7
Finance and insurance	3.6	3.6	3.6	5.5	5.3	5.7
Real estate	4.8	5.2	4.1	1.9	1.7	2.2
Services	3.7	3.5	4.3	3.8	3.7	4.1

	Labor input			Total factor input		
	1948-76	1948-66	1966-76	1948-76	1948-66	1966-76
Mining	-0.3	-2.0	2.8	0.1	-1.1	2.3
Contract construction	1.4	1.8	0.7	1.6	2.0	0.9
Total transportation	-0.5	-0.9	0.3	-0.3	-0.5	0.3
Railroad	-3.7	-4.3	-2.5	-3.1	-3.6	-2.2
Nonrail	1.2	1.2	1.2	1.6	1.7	1.3
Communications	2.0	0.4	2.7	2.8	1.9	4.3
Public utilities	0.9	0.4	1.8	2.7	2.2	3.6
Trade	1.3	1.1	1.8	1.6	1.4	2.7
Finance and insurance	2.1	2.8	3.8	3.5	3.2	4.0
Real estate	2.5	1.8	3.6	1.9	1.8	2.3
Services	1.7	1.5	2.0	3.8	1.9	2.4

	Total factor productivity			Output/labor ratio		
	1948-76	1948-66	1966-76	1948-76	1948-66	1966-76
Mining	1.7	3.3	-1.2	2.1	4.2	-1.7
Contract construction	1.0	2.5	-1.6	1.2	2.7	-1.5
Total transportation	2.4	2.9	1.6	2.6	3.2	1.5
Railroad	2.5	4.2	-0.6	3.1	5.0	-0.2
Nonrail	1.8	1.6	2.0	2.2	2.2	2.2
Communications	4.2	4.7	3.3	5.8	6.3	4.9
Public utilities	3.0	4.9	-0.3	4.8	6.8	1.5
Trade	2.1	2.5	1.4	2.4	2.8	1.6
Finance and insurance	0.1	0.4	-0.4	0.5	0.8	-0.1
Real estate	2.8	3.4	1.8	2.3	3.3	0.5
Services	1.6	1.5	1.8	2.0	1.9	2.3

	Output/capital ratio			Capital/labor ratio		
	1948-76	1948-66	1966-76	1948-76	1948-66	1966-76
Mining	1.0	1.7	-0.3	1.1	2.4	-1.3
Contract construction	-2.3	-1.8	-3.2	3.5	4.5	1.7
Total transportation	1.4	1.2	1.8	1.2	2.0	-0.3
Railroad	-0.6	0.3	-2.1	3.7	4.7	1.9
Nonrail	-0.7	-1.9	1.5	2.9	4.1	0.7
Communications	1.3	1.0	1.7	4.5	5.2	3.2
Public utilities	1.4	3.0	-1.3	3.4	3.7	2.8
Trade	0.3	0.2	0.6	2.0	2.7	0.9
Finance and insurance	-1.8	-1.6	-2.0	2.3	2.5	1.9
Real estate	2.9	3.4	1.9	-0.6	-0.1	-1.4
Services	-0.1	-0.2	0.2	2.1	2.1	2.1

a healthy increase in its capital-labor ratio of 3.7 percent per year, and productivity in this industry grew at a 2.5 percent rate, the fourth highest among industries in this sector. Obviously, slow growth or even decline in output does not necessarily imply slow or negative rates of productivity advance.

The greatest gain in TFP was in the communications industry at a 4.2 average percent annual rate. This fast pace reflects, in part, the high rate of capital infusion averaging 5.8 percent per year, and a 4.5 percent rate of increase in its capital-labor ratio. This fast gain in productivity reflects the tremendous technological advances that were developed during and after World War II. Another industry that had substantial gains in productivity (3 percent rate) due to new technologies is the public utilities industry.

In contrast is the real estate industry, which ranked third in productivity gains (2.8 percent rate) within this sector. Its capital-labor ratio actually declined at a 0.6 percent rate—another example that not all productivity gains are due to embodied technological advances. On the other end of the spectrum is the finance and insurance industry, which had a very high growth in both capital and labor inputs, yet exhibited virtually no gain in productivity after 1948, although this largely reflects the method of estimating output.

Manufacturing

The manufacturing sector, composed of twenty two-digit SIC industries, represents about 29 percent[6] of the gross product of the private domestic business economy in 1976. Because of the tremendous variation in type of production, capital intensity, and other factors that underlie economic growth within this sector, much of the causal analysis in this study concentrates on the manufacturing industries.

Table 3-5 presents the postwar growth rates of output, capital, and labor inputs, and TFP for the twenty manufacturing industries. The rates of change of output vary from a high of 6.4 percent in the electrical equipment industry to a decline in output at the rate of 0.2 percent exhibited by the leather industry. Most of the high growth industries appear to be capital-intensive or high-technology in nature. The top ranking industries in terms of their growth rates of output are chemicals, instruments, and transportation equipment.

---

[6]As measured by shares of constant 1972 dollar output. The nonfarm-nonmanufacturing sector represents 68 percent, and farm 3 percent. These compare to shares of 30 percent, 64 percent, and 6 percent in 1948 for the manufacturing, nonfarm-nonmanufacturing, and farm sectors, respectively.

Table 3-5. Trends of outputs, inputs, and productivity for manufacturing industries
(percent changes at annual rates)

	Output			Capital input		
	1948-76	1948-66	1966-76	1948-76	1948-66	1966-76
Food	2.7	2.9	2.4	0.8	0.7	1.0
Tobacco	2.4	2.2	2.6	1.0	1.1	0.8
Textiles	2.7	3.5	1.4	3.1	4.1	1.5
Apparel	3.0	3.1	2.8	2.5	1.6	4.1
Lumber	2.3	2.3	2.3	0.3	-2.0	4.6
Furniture	2.7	3.4	1.6	1.4	0.7	2.6
Paper	3.8	4.4	2.7	2.8	3.0	2.6
Printing and publishing	2.9	3.8	1.2	2.2	1.5	3.6
Chemicals	5.8	6.7	4.0	3.9	4.6	2.7
Petroleum	3.5	3.9	2.8	2.7	2.6	2.9
Rubber	4.7	5.5	3.3	3.9	3.8	4.1
Leather	-0.2	0.6	-1.5	0.5	0.1	1.3
Stone, clay, and glass	2.5	3.3	0.9	3.3	3.9	2.1
Primary metals	0.6	2.1	-2.0	3.1	3.6	2.0
Fabricated metals	3.0	4.1	1.1	4.5	5.2	3.2
Equipment, excluding electrical	3.1	3.8	1.9	4.1	4.1	4.2
Electrical equipment	6.4	8.2	3.2	4.5	4.7	4.0
Transportation equipment	4.8	6.7	1.4	3.8	4.3	2.8
Instruments	5.4	6.6	3.1	5.4	5.9	4.6
Miscellaneous manufactures	2.8	2.9	2.7	1.3	0.3	3.2
Total manufacturing	3.3	4.2	1.8	3.0	3.1	2.8

Table 3-5. Trends of outputs, inputs, and productivity for manufacturing industries (percent changes at annual rates) (cont.)

	Labor input			Total factor input		
	1948-76	1948-66	1966-76	1948-76	1948-66	1966-76
Food	-0.4	-0.4	-0.5	-0.1	-0.1	-0.2
Tobacco	-1.5	-1.6	-1.2	-0.2	-0.3	0.0
Textiles	-1.1	-1.5	-0.3	-0.3	-0.5	0.1
Apparel	0.2	0.9	-1.0	0.5	0.9	-0.3
Lumber	-1.2	-1.6	-0.5	-0.6	-1.6	1.4
Furniture	0.8	1.3	-0.0	0.9	1.2	0.3
Paper	1.2	1.9	-0.0	1.7	2.2	0.8
Printing and publishing	1.0	1.4	0.5	1.3	1.4	1.1
Chemicals	1.6	2.1	0.7	2.5	3.1	1.5
Petroleum	-0.3	-1.0	0.9	1.4	1.0	2.2
Rubber	2.5	3.1	1.6	2.9	3.2	2.2
Leather	-1.5	-0.6	-3.2	-1.2	-0.5	-2.5
Stone, clay, and glass	0.5	0.9	-0.4	1.1	1.6	0.3
Primary metals	-0.3	0.4	-1.5	0.5	1.2	-0.6
Fabricated metals	1.2	1.9	-0.0	1.8	2.4	0.6
Equipment, excluding electrical	1.4	2.1	0.3	2.0	2.5	1.2
Electrical equipment	2.2	3.8	-0.6	2.7	3.9	0.4
Transportation equipment	1.5	3.1	-1.5	2.0	3.4	-0.4
Instruments	2.3	2.9	1.3	3.0	3.5	2.3
Miscellaneous manufactures	-0.2	0.0	-0.6	0.1	0.1	0.1
Total manufacturing	0.6	1.2	-0.4	1.2	1.6	0.5

	Total factor productivity			Output/labor ratio		
	1948-76	1948-66	1966-76	1948-76	1948-66	1966-76
Mining	1.7	3.3	-1.2	2.1	4.2	-1.7
Contract construction	1.0	2.5	-1.6	1.2	2.7	-1.5
Total transportation	2.4	2.9	1.6	2.6	3.2	1.5
Railroad	2.5	4.2	-0.6	3.1	5.0	-0.2
Nonrail	1.8	1.6	2.0	2.2	2.2	2.2
Communications	4.2	4.7	3.3	5.8	6.3	4.9
Public utilities	3.0	4.9	-0.3	4.8	6.8	1.5
Trade	2.1	2.5	1.4	2.4	2.8	1.6
Finance and insurance	0.1	0.4	-0.4	0.5	0.8	-0.1
Real estate	2.8	3.4	1.8	2.3	3.3	0.5
Services	1.6	1.5	1.8	2.0	1.9	2.3

	Output/capital ratio			Capital/labor ratio		
	1948-76	1948-66	1966-76	1948-76	1948-66	1966-76
Mining	1.0	1.7	-0.3	1.1	2.4	-1.3
Contract construction	-2.3	-1.8	-3.2	3.5	4.5	1.7
Total transportation	1.4	1.2	1.8	1.2	2.0	-0.3
Railroad	-0.6	0.3	-2.1	3.7	4.7	1.9
Nonrail	-0.7	-1.9	1.5	2.9	4.1	0.7
Communications	1.3	1.0	1.7	4.5	5.2	3.2
Public utilities	1.4	3.0	-1.3	3.4	3.7	2.8
Trade	0.3	0.2	0.6	2.0	2.7	0.9
Finance and insurance	-1.8	-1.6	-2.0	2.3	2.5	1.9
Real estate	2.9	3.4	1.9	-0.6	-0.1	-1.4
Services	-0.1	-0.2	0.2	2.1	2.1	2.1

Table 3-6. Capital per person engaged, 1948, 1966, and 1976
(thousands of 1972 dollars and average annual percentage rates of change)

	Capital per person (thousands of 72$)			Rate of change (percent)		
	1948	1966	1976	1948-76	1948-66	1966-76
Mining	36.9	61.8	57.8	1.6	2.9	-0.7
Contract construction	3.6	7.9	9.3	3.4	4.4	1.7
Railroad transportation	127.1	279.2	353.9	3.7	4.5	2.4
Nonrail transportation	18.8	33.3	35.6	2.3	3.2	0.7
Communications	42.5	95.6	137.9	4.3	4.6	3.7
Public utilities	151.9	265.3	364.5	3.2	3.1	3.2
Trade	8.7	12.6	13.1	1.5	2.1	0.4
Finance and insurance	10.0	15.3	19.4	2.4	2.4	2.4
Real estate	698.6	664.7	589.9	-0.6	-0.3	-1.2
Services	13.5	16.6	18.9	1.2	1.2	1.3
Nonfarm-nonmanufacturing	34.8	41.0	43.3	0.8	0.9	0.6
Food	18.3	21.3	24.6	1.1	0.9	1.4
Tobacco	29.9	48.6	58.7	2.4	2.7	1.9
Textiles	5.6	16.1	18.5	4.3	6.0	1.4
Apparel	3.3	3.7	6.1	2.2	0.8	5.0

Lumber	12.4	11.4	18.1	1.4	-0.5	4.8
Furniture	9.1	8.0	9.8	0.3	-0.7	2.1
Paper	30.1	56.2	46.2	1.5	1.0	2.5
Printing and publishing	11.2	11.0	14.6	1.0	-0.1	2.9
Chemicals	29.0	25.3	55.0	2.3	2.5	2.0
Petroleum	62.9	124.6	150.9	3.2	3.9	1.9
Rubber	13.8	16.6	20.8	1.5	1.0	2.3
Leather	4.0	4.7	7.1	2.1	0.9	4.3
Stone, clay, and glass	16.4	28.3	35.8	2.8	3.1	2.4
Primary metals	26.0	47.2	65.5	3.4	3.4	3.3
Fabricated metals	8.8	16.0	21.4	3.2	3.4	2.9
Machinery, excluding electric	12.7	18.8	26.1	2.6	2.2	3.4
Electrical machinery	9.8	11.7	18.1	2.2	1.0	4.4
Transportation equipment	13.7	17.9	27.1	2.5	1.5	4.2
Instruments	8.4	14.5	19.3	3.0	3.1	2.9
Miscellaneous manufactures	10.1	10.5	14.7	1.3	0.2	3.4
Manufacturing	14.4	20.6	27.4	2.3	2.0	2.9

Yet, in terms of real capital per employee in 1976 (Table 3-6), these industries ranked fourth, thirteenth, and ninth, respectively. Just as capital intensity cannot explain high growth rates of output, neither can the rates of changes in capital inputs. In this regard, chemicals, instruments, and transportation equipment ranked sixth, first, and seventh, respectively.

Factors underlying growth rates in output include, among other things, changes in relative prices which, in turn, reflect relative changes in demand and TFP. There is a fairly close relationship between productivity growth rates and rates of change in output (Table 3-5). Two of the top three industries in terms of productivity also achieved the highest growth in output. However, textiles, whose productivity ranked third, ranked fifteenth in terms of output.[7]

In contrast, there is no strong relationship between rates of changes in capital per employee and productivity (Table 3-6). The electrical equipment industry, which achieved the highest gain in productivity, increased its capital per employee at a rate of 2.2 percent. Yet the primary metals industry had a 3.4 percent rate of gain in its capital per employee, but only a negligible rise in its productivity.

Figure 3-3 shows the dispersion in the 1948-76 rates of change in total and partial factor productivity. The TFP of most industries is between 1.0 and 2.9 percent. Only one industry, primary metals, had less than a 1.0 percent gain. The partial labor productivity measure exhibits a very similar dispersion, except that the bulk of rates of change are over 2 percent. In contrast, the output per unit of capital measure exhibits a less upward skewed dispersion and includes slower gains. In fact, seven industries had declines in their output-capital ratios, in contrast to only positive rates for the other productivity measures.

Even though all of the manufacturing industries exhibited positive advances in productivity over the postwar period, this is not the case for subperiods as shown by Table 3-7. Here, too, the cyclical peak years were chosen, except for 1976, to minimize the impact of underutilization of capital on the productivity estimates. Except for the long 1960-66 expansion, in each of the subperiods at least one industry experienced a decline in its productivity. Although eight industries showed declines in productivity from 1973 to 1976, when the estimates can be extended through the peak of the current cycle, most of the industries will be seen to have experienced productivity gains.

The variation in productivity growth rates is quite striking. For example, the lumber industry, which ranked fourth in terms of its 1948-76 produc-

[7]This close relationship between productivity and output is to be expected. See Chapter 6 for further discussion on this point.

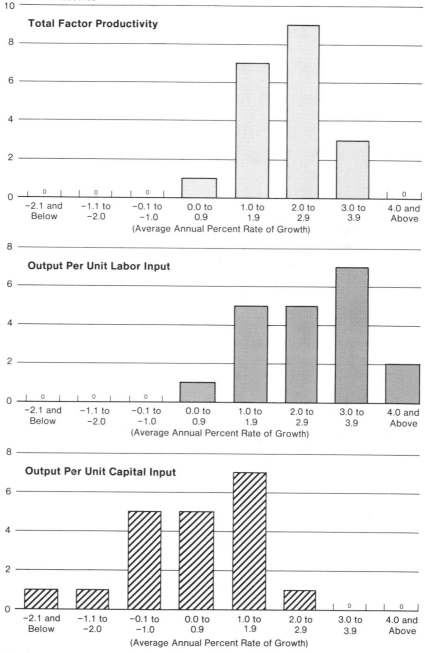

Figure 3-3. Dispersion of 20 manufacturing industries' average annual rates of change of total and partial factor productivity, 1948-76

Sources: U.S. Department of Labor; U.S. Department of Commerce; Conference Board.

Table 3-7. Twenty manufacturing industries: total factor productivity, 1948-76, by subperiod
(average annual percentage rates of change)

	1948-53	1953-57	1957-60	1960-66	1966-69	1969-73	1973-76	1948-76
Manufacturing	2.9	1.0	1.1	3.9	0.9	2.7	0.1	2.1
Food	3.3	2.5	1.1	4.0	1.1	2.8	3.7	2.9
Tobacco	1.1	3.5	4.8	2.0	3.6	3.0	1.1	2.6
Textiles	0.8	3.6	1.9	8.2	0.1	2.7	0.7	3.1
Apparel	2.8	1.4	1.9	2.0	0.8	5.5	2.5	2.5
Lumber	0.4	5.8	1.5	7.2	1.6	4.9	-4.7	2.9
Furniture	2.2	2.7	0.1	2.7	2.0	1.0	0.8	1.8
Paper	3.7	-0.4	1.7	2.8	2.7	5.3	-3.5	2.0
Printing and publishing	2.2	2.8	0.6	3.1	0.2	0.7	-1.0	1.5
Chemicals	1.8	4.3	2.5	5.0	2.9	4.7	-0.9	3.2
Petroleum	1.8	0.6	5.4	4.1	0.8	2.3	-1.7	2.1
Rubber	2.1	-2.4	5.7	3.6	3.2	1.4	-1.5	1.8
Leather	-2.0	0.7	3.0	3.1	-0.3	2.1	1.2	1.1
Stone, clay, and glass	2.4	0.1	1.1	2.4	0.8	1.7	-0.9	1.3
Primary metals	3.2	-1.5	-4.1	3.3	-3.1	1.8	-3.9	0.1
Fabricated metals	1.4	0.3	2.0	2.6	1.5	0.9	-0.9	1.3
Machinery, excluding electric	2.5	-1.9	1.1	2.6	-0.2	2.3	-0.5	1.1
Electrical machinery	4.4	2.0	2.6	6.2	2.9	3.7	1.6	3.7
Transportation equipment	3.2	1.5	3.3	4.2	-0.5	2.7	3.0	2.7
Instruments	4.6	0.6	3.0	3.5	3.1	-0.4	0.1	2.2
Miscellaneous manufactures	4.0	3.3	2.6	1.6	3.1	2.8	1.6	2.7

Source: The Conference Board.

tivity growth of 2.9 percent, achieved a 7.2 percent rate of gain in the 1960-66 period. During the 1969-73 period, a 4.9 percent rise in productivity was achieved, but this gain was followed by a 4.7 percent rate of *decline* between 1973 and 1976. This latter period covers, of course, the worst postwar recession. Since 1976 is not a peak year, the 1973-76 period is not consistent with the other subperiods. Nevertheless, it is noteworthy that half of the industries experienced declines in their productivity between 1973 and 1976.

The Post-1966 Slowdown in Total Factor Productivity

Evidence of a slowdown in the growth of TFP for the overall economy is well established. Between 1948 and 1966 productivity, as measured for the private domestic business economy, grew at a 2.9 percent annual rate, but over the 1966-76 subperiod productivity rose at only half this rate, 1.4 percent. This slowdown is reflected in all three sectors; its likely causes are examined elsewhere[8] (Chapters 2 and 6). However, not all industries have experienced a slowdown in their productvity growth since the mid-1960s. In this section, the productivity trends by industry are examined to determine which industries have experienced a slowdown, or possibly an acceleration, in their productivity trends. First, each sector and industry is examined graphically; then, using regression analysis, the industries having a statistically significant shift in their post-1966 productivity trends will be pinpointed.

Figures 3-1 and 3-2 show the trends of TFP for the private domestic business economy and its three sectors. For the economy as a whole, the slowdown appears to have begun about 1968. On a sector basis, the farm sector does not exhibit a slowdown until 1971, while the nonfarm-nonmanufacturing sector shows a slowdown in its productivity trend beginning about 1968. The manufacturing sector exhibits a productivity slowdown starting in 1966.

Within the nonfarm-nonmanufacturing sector, five industry groups have incurred a slowdown in their productivity growth rates: mining, since 1970; contract construction, since 1968; railroad transportation, since 1966; public utilities, since 1966; and trade, since 1968. The other industries' productivity trends continued at the same rate over the two subperiods, except for finance and insurance, for which the productivity estimates are not meaningful.

There was great variability in TFP trends within the manufacturing sector. Some of the industries, such as food, exhibit smooth growth in produc-

[8]Council of Economic Advisers, *Economic Report to the President* (Washington, D.C.: U.S. Government Printing Office, 1977), pp. 45-48.

tivity, whereas others, such as primary metals, have no discernible trends. For such industry patterns as exhibited by primary metals, using the compound interest formula to calculate productivity growth rates may result in misleading estimates. Further, even if such calculations were fairly representative, it is not possible to compare statistically the growth rates of two sub-periods (i.e., 1948-66 and 1966-76) and state whether there is a significant difference between them. To overcome these two problems, regression analysis was applied to the sectors and the manufacturing industries.

The type of model[9] applied here allows for a shift in the productivity trend by incorporating a dummy variable that is equal to zero from 1948 to 1965 and one thereafter. The coefficient of the dummy variable indicates whether or not the shift in the trend is statistically significant, as well as the change in the percentage growth rate. Further, accounting for the impact of variations in capacity utilization may be accomplished by including such a measure in the regression model. Table 3-8 presents the results of this model applied to the major sectors and the manufacturing industries.

Of the major sectors, the farm and manufacturing sectors showed no statistically significant decline in their productivity trends since 1966, as did the private domestic business economy, nonfarm-nonmanufacturing, and non-financial business sectors. Even though the manufacturing sector as a whole showed no significant shift in its productivity trend, eight of the twenty manufacturing industries had statistically significant declines in their trends over the 1966-76 decade. Two industries, apparel and paper, had significant increases in their rates of productivity growth after 1966.

The lumber industry had the largest decline in its trend, a fall-off of 3.5 percentage points from 3.9 percent between 1948 and 1966 to 0.4 percent during the following subperiod. One industry, primary metals, had no significant trend in its productivity during either of the two subperiods. Most of the growth rates estimated by the regression model are close to the rates calculated by the compound method (Tables 3-2 and 3-5).

The intensity in the use of real capital stock (i.e., capacity utilization) has an impact on productivity. As the economy expands, more of the capital stock is utilized and, to meet ever greater demands, less efficient capital must be called into service. Other inefficiencies in the use of capital also crop up as utilization intensifies. Further, during periods of slower economic activity, the existing capital stock must be maintained, thereby lowering the output-capital ratio. To account for the impact of the utilization of capital on estimates of productivity growth rates, the capacity utilization rate for each in-

---

[9]Manoranjan Dutta, *Econometric Methods* (Cincinnati: South-Western Publishing Co., 1975), pp. 177-78.

Table 3-8. *Shifts in rates of growth of total factor productivity, 1948-66 to 1966-76 (average annual percentage rates of change)*

	1948-66 rates of growth	1966-76 shift in rates	1966-76 derived rates	Impact of capacity utilization
Private domestic business	2.65	−1.23*	1.42	0.10
Nonfinancial corporate business	2.43*	−1.00*	1.43	0.23
Farming	3.68*	−1.52	2.16	−
Nonfarm-nonmanufacturing	2.35*	−1.47*	0.88	−
Manufacturing	2.11*	−0.42	1.69	0.34*
Food	2.90*	−0.70*	2.20	0.00
Tobacco	2.63*	0.00	2.63	0.00
Textiles	3.89*	−2.20*	1.69	0.00
Apparel	1.64*	1.89*	3.55	0.04
Lumber	3.93*	−3.50*	0.43	0.13*
Furniture	1.72*	−0.40	1.32	0.03
Paper	1.37*	1.31*	2.68	0.05
Printing and publishing	2.14*	−2.26*	−0.12	0.00
Chemicals	3.43*	−0.85	2.59	0.00
Petroleum	2.97*	−2.40*	0.57	0.09
Rubber	1.97*	−0.98	0.99	0.13
Leather	1.47*	−0.56	0.91	−0.06
Stone, clay, and glass	1.52*	−1.02*	0.50	0.10*
Primary metals	0.22	−0.61	−0.41	0.33*
Fabricated metals	1.45*	−1.13*	0.32	0.05*
Machinery, excluding electrical	0.83*	−0.07	0.76	0.09
Electrical equipment	3.55*	−0.63	2.92	0.13
Transportation equipment	2.52*	−0.48	2.04	0.94*
Instruments	2.45*	−1.82*	0.63	0.06
Miscellaneous manufactures	3.02*	−0.67	2.35	0.01

*Significant at the 0.05 level.

Note: Based on the regression, LOG (total factor productivity) $= a + b*$Trend $+ c*$Trend$*D66 + d*D66 + e*(1/[1$-capacity utilization rate]) for 1948-76; $D66$ equals 0 from 1948 to 1965 and 1 thereafter; column 1 equals estimate of b times 100; column 2 equals estimate of c times 100; column 3 equals column 1 plus column 2; column 4 equals estimate of e times 100; capacity utilization rate from Wharton Econometric Forecasting Unit; capacity utilization rates equal to 1.00 are adjusted to 0.99.

Sources: Wharton Econometric Forecasting Unit; The Conference Board.

dustry was included in the regression model. Since capacity pressures become considerably more critical as capacity ceilings are approached, the capacity utilization rate is entered in an inverse form: one over one minus the capacity utilization rate. Therefore, a positive coefficient with respect to this variable would indicate a negative relationship with productivity.

Capacity utilization has a significant, negative impact on productivity trends in the private domestic business economy, nonfinancial corporate business, and manufacturing sectors. (No capacity utilization rate was included in the farm or nonfarm-nonmanufacturing sectors.) Within manufacturing, five industries exhibited significant, negative impacts of capacity utilization on their productivity trends: lumber; stone, clay, and glass; primary metals; fabricated metals; and transportation equipment. All of these industries are highly cyclical in nature, as indicated by the significant role played by the capacity utilization rate variable. The role of variations in this rate in explaining differences in productivity growth rates across industries is explored more fully in Chapter 6.

CHAPTER 4

Productivity, Costs, and Prices

In addition to its role as the major source of rising planes of living, productivity is also a potent counterinflationary force. This is so since productivity increases offset to a greater or lesser degree the effect of rising factor prices on unit costs, which are the main element in product prices.

In the analysis for this chapter, we look first at the nonfinancial corporate sector before going on to the total business economy by major industry groups. This is done for two reasons. In the corporate sector, it is not necessary to split net proprietors' income between labor and property compensation, since the sector excludes unincorporated businesses. Second, the Bureau of Economic Analysis provides estimates of the capital consumption adjustment (CCA) for revaluation of nonfinancial corporate profits that makes possible a more meaningful breakdown of gross property income between net income (profit) and fixed capital costs (depreciation and interest). The following discussion, however, is based primarily on property income estimates without adjustment of capital consumption to replacement cost in order to provide comparability with the industry estimates for which CCA is not available. But we shall also indicate the general effect of CCA for the sector on unit profits and capital consumption allowances.

We look first at the entire period 1948-76, then at the 1948-66 and 1966-76 subperiods. The latter decade is of particular interest because of the slowdown in productivity growth and the concomitant marked acceleration of inflation. If we had pushed the estimates to 1978, the rate of productivity growth would be further reduced and the inflation rate raised.

51

In what follows, while we decompose changes in product price into their major cost components in order to observe the counterinflationary role of productivity change, we do not mean to imply that price inflation is exclusively the result of cost-push forces. In periods of strong increases of money demand associated with rising profit margins, the presumption is that demand-pull forces are also operating. In other periods, cost-push may be operating more strongly. Our objective is not to analyze the causes of inflation. Rather, it is to show the extent to which increases in unit cost and prices have been mitigated by increasing productivity. Our estimates of capital and TFP (total factor productivity) make possible a more complete analysis than can be done on the basis of the official estimates, which are limited to real product per labor hour.

The Nonfinancial Corporate Sector

Trends between 1948 and 1976.   Prices rose almost 3 percent a year, on average, between 1948 and 1976 in the nonfinancial corporate sector, which accounts for more than half of gross business product. But if TFP had remained constant instead of rising at an average annual rate of 2.2 percent over the same period, prices would have risen by almost 5 percent a year, on average, other things being equal. Thus, productivity growth offset about 40 percent of the increase in unit cost that would have occurred in its absence if nothing else had changed.

The arithmetic of this and other calculations shown in the tables is relatively simple. The rate of change in the price index (implicit price deflator for gross product of the sector) is in effect a weighted average of the rates of change in the component indexes of unit cost, including profits. The weights are the proportions of the several cost categories of gross product in the first of the two years between which rates of change are computed. These proportions are shown in Table 4-1 below for the years 1948 and 1966, which are the beginning years for rate-of-change computations, plus 1976, in order to show the trends in the cost proportions over the entire period. Thus, we see that indirect business taxes less subsidies, etc. rose from 8.8 percent of gross product in 1948 to 10 percent in 1976, while factor cost dropped correspondingly from 91.2 percent to 90 percent. An increasing proportion means that the component's unit cost (cost divided by real product) rose more than the gross product price deflator, and vice versa. Thus, unit indirect business taxes rose by 3.42 percent a year, on average, compared with a 2.97 average annual percentage increase in the price defla-

Table 4-1. Gross product of the U.S. nonfinancial corporate business sector, composition by cost categories, 1948, 1966, and 1976
(billions of dollars and percentages)

	1948		1966		1976	
	Billions of dollars	Percentages	Billions of dollars	Percentages	Billions of dollars	Percentages
Gross product originating	137.3	100.0	430.7	100.0	991.0	100.0
Indirect business taxes, etc.	12.1	8.8	42.9	10.0	99.4	10.0
Factor costs, total	125.2	91.2	387.8	90.0	891.6	90.0
Labor compensation	87.8	64.0	273.5	63.5	650.3	65.6
Property compensation	37.4	27.2	114.3	26.5	241.3	24.3
Corporate profits:						
with IVA & CCA	25.8	18.8	71.2	16.5	101.9	10.3
(with IVA only)	(29.7)	(21.6)	(67.4)	(15.6)	(116.4)	(11.7)
Fixed capital costs:						
with CCA	11.6	8.4	43.1	10.0	139.4	14.1
(without CCA)	(7.7)	(5.6)	(46.9)	(10.9)	(124.9)	(12.6)
Capital consumption:						
with CCA	10.7	7.8	35.7	8.3	107.0	10.8
(without CCA)	(6.8)	(5.0)	(39.5)	(9.2)	(92.5)	(9.3)
Net interest	0.9	0.7	7.4	1.7	32.4	3.3

Note: The figures in parentheses show corporate profits, fixed capital costs, and capital consumption allowances without capital consumption adjustments to replacement costs in order to provide comparability with the estimates for the business sector industry groups for which the CCA is not available.
Sources: Bureau of Economic Analysis, U.S. Department of Commerce.

tor and, therefore, the tax share rose. Unit factor costs rose by 2.92 percent a year, and the factor income share declined. The price deflator's rate of change equals a weighted average of the component unit cost changes (3.42 x .088 + 2.92 x .912 = 2.97).

Labor compensation rose slightly from 64 percent of gross product in 1948 to 65.6 percent in 1976. The relative increase was somewhat larger as a proportion of total factor cost, of course. Property compensation declined from 27.2 percent of gross product in 1948 to 24.4 percent in 1976. It is within this category that the relative movements are most divergent. Unit fixed capital costs (without CCA) climbed from 5.6 percent to 12.6 percent over the twenty-eight year period. But the proportionate rise in the small net interest component from 0.7 percent to 3.3 percent was far greater than the rise in capital consumption allowances from 5 percent to 9.3 percent. Corporate profits before tax plummeted from 21.6 percent in 1948 to 11.7 percent in 1976—most of the drop coming after 1966.

The capital consumption adjustments to replacement cost valuation (CCA) increased capital consumption in both 1948 and 1976 and decreased profits correspondingly. But the adjustment was a larger percentage of gross product in 1948 than in 1976, so the proportionate increase in capital consumption with CCA was less than without it, and the proportionate decline in corporate profits was less. In 1966, however, the CCA was negative, so capital consumption with CCA rose much less from 1948 to 1966 than without it, and much more from 1966 to 1976. Conversely, corporate profits with CCA dropped less from 1948 to 1966 than without the adjustment, and more from 1966 to 1976. These differences should be kept in mind in the following discussion, which relates to the capital consumption and profit estimates without the CCA.

We can now examine the trends in unit factor costs shown in Table 4-2, with particular respect to the ameliorative impact of productivity. Here it is important to keep in mind that the rate of change in unit factor cost (2.92) approximately equals the *difference* between the rates of change in average factor price and in productivity (5.16-2.18). The fact that this difference, 2.98, is a little higher than the 2.92 rate of change in unit factor cost reflects the multiplicative nature of the relationship. That is, factor costs (C_F) per unit of output (O) equals the quotient of factor cost per unit of input (C_F/I, which is the average factor price) and total factor productivity: $C_F/O = C_F/I \div O/I$. By adding 100.00 to the rates of change of these variables, we see that $105.16 \div 102.18 = 102.92$ precisely. But in view of the small discrepancy between the quotient less 100.00 and the differences between rates of change, we can estimate the productivity impact as the quotient of the

*Table 4-2. U.S. nonfinancial corporate business sector,
components of price change, 1948-76*

	1948 relative weights (percentages)	Average annual percentage rates of change	Contributions to price change Percentage points	Percent
Implicit price deflator	100.0	2.97	2.97	100.0
Unit indirect business taxes	8.8	3.42	0.30	10.1
Unit factor cost	91.2	2.92	2.66	89.9
Average factor price		5.16	4.71	158.6
Total factor productivity		2.18	−1.99	−67.0
Unit labor cost	63.9	3.07	1.96	66.2
Average hourly compensation		5.78	3.69	124.2
Real product per hour		2.64	−1.69	−56.9
Unit capital cost	27.3	2.55	0.70	23.6
Average price of capital		3.46	0.94	31.6
Real product per unit of capital		0.90	−0.24	−8.1
Unit fixed capital cost	5.6	5.94		
Unit depreciation	5.0	5.29		
Unit net interest	0.7	8.94		
Unit profits	21.6	0.75		

average percentage change in productivity and the average percentage change in factor price obtained as the sum of the rates of change in productivity and in unit factor cost. On this basis, we calculate that productivity growth offset 42.6 percent of the increase in unit cost [2.18 ÷(2.18 + 2.92)].

The same approach can be used to explain changes in the two major components of unit factor cost. Thus, the 3.07 average annual percentage rate of change in unit labor cost reflects the 5.78 rate of increase in average hourly labor compensation, less the 2.64 rate of growth of labor productivity. (More precisely, 105.78 ÷ 102.64 = 103.06.) So the increase in labor productivity offset about 46 percent of the impact of increasing average hourly earnings on unit labor costs. Note that when the increase in average hourly labor earnings is deflated by the price index, real average compensation is seen to increase by 2.7 percent a year. This is slightly more than the 2.6 percent increase in labor productivity, a necessary condition for a rising labor share of gross factor income.

Note also that as shown in the last two columns of Table 4-2, increasing unit labor costs contributed almost two percentage points to the 3 percent inflation rate between 1948 and 1976. The 67 percent contribution of labor to the price rise was greater than its 64 percent share of gross product in 1948, which is consistent with the rising share of labor through 1976.

The 2.55 percent average increase in unit capital costs (including profit) is roughly equal to the 3.44 increase in the average price of capital less the 0.85 rise in capital productivity. When the average price of capital—which reflects both the price of capital goods and the rate of return on capital—is deflated by the product price index, the real price of capital rises by 0.47 percent a year, on average. This is less than the increase in capital productivity, and it is this difference that contributed to the rising share of labor. Rising unit capital costs contributed about 0.7, or 23 percent, of the 3 percent inflation rate between 1948 and 1976. This was less than the 27 percent property share of gross product in 1948, which is consistent with the declining trend of that share from 1948 to 1976, as shown in Table 4-1.

It is of interest to look at the behavior of the components of unit capital cost, although the productivity offset cannot be split up correspondingly. Net interest per unit of output rose at an 8.9 percent average annual rate and unit depreciation at a 5.3 percent rate, while unit profits increased by only 0.75 percent a year, on average. While the rising fixed capital costs per unit of output contributed 0.33 percentage point, or 11 percent of the 3 percent a year price rise in the period 1948-76, unit profits contributed only 0.16, or about 5 percent of the inflation rate.

Balance sheet data in conjunction with the income flows make possible a more detailed analysis of changes in unit property costs in terms of rates of return on assets and on net worth in the financial noncorporate sector. But we shall defer this until we look at the differences in movements of unit costs in the two subperiods.

Subperiod Trends, 1948-1966 and 1966-1976.   During the eighteen-year period 1948-66 the price index for gross product originating in nonfinancial corporations rose at an average annual rate of about 1.7 percent; in the following decade the rate of price inflation accelerated sharply to over 5.3 percent (Table 4-3). In part, this was due to the deceleration in the trend rate of productivity advance of more than half, from 2.65 percent to 1.32 percent a year. If there had been no productivity growth in both subperiods, prices would have risen by 4.15 percent during 1948-66, and by 6.5 percent in the subsequent decade, other things equal. Thus, productivity offset 64 percent of the hypothetical price rise in the earlier subperiod, but only about 20 percent in the decade 1966-76. Of course, other things are not equal. It is quite possible that the much lower productivity advance in the decade 1966-76, which was associated with retardation of increases in real wages, may have contributed to the acceleration of factor prices, as workers sought larger increases in nominal average earnings gains.

Of the cost components, it is interesting that average increases in unit indirect business taxes less subsidies, etc., at 2.4 percent a year during 1948-66 and 5.3 percent during 1966-76, exceeded the increases in prices in the earlier period, but merely kept pace with other unit costs in the latter period. The successful effort by governments to increase their real revenues from this source in relation to real product contributed about 12.5 percent of the inflation rate in the first subperiod, and 10 percent in the second.

Unit factor cost increased by almost as much as prices in the first subperiod and at the same rate in the second. But between 1948 and 1966, the 2.65 percent average annual growth in TFP provided a 62 percent offset to the 4.3 percent increase in average factor prices; while in the subsequent decade the 1.32 average increase in productivity offset the 6.7 percent a year average increase in factor prices by less than 20 percent.

Looking at the cost components, average hourly labor compensation rose at an average rate of 4.8 percent a year during 1948-66, accelerating to 7.6 percent in the following subperiod. In the initial subperiod, average growth in real product per labor hour of 3.1 percent a year represented almost two-thirds of the wage-rate gain, reducing the average increase in unit labor costs to 1.65 percent a year. In the second subperiod, labor productivity gains averaging 1.82 percent a year offset less than one-quarter of the wage-rate gains with respect to their impact on unit labor costs, which rose at an average annual rate of 5.66 percent. As a result, the increase in unit labor costs accounted for a larger fraction of the inflation rate in the second subperiod than in the first—67.7 percent compared with 62.7 percent.

The average price of capital rose by over 2.9 percent a year during 1948-66 and by almost 4.4 percent in the following decade, but in the first subperiod, growth in capital productivity averaging 1.35 percent a year meant that unit capital compensation rose by only 1.5 percent a year. In the second subperiod, there was virtually no capital productivity offset, as real capital stocks grew practically as fast as real product, so unit capital charges rose by slightly over 4.4 percent a year, on average. But in both subperiods the increase in unit capital costs was less than price increases and contributed 24 percent to the inflation rate in the first and 22 percent in the second.

The component holding down the increase in unit capital costs, particularly in the second subperiod, was profits. Unit profits (with CCA) sagged slightly in the first subperiod, shading the inflation rate. In the second subperiod, unit profits declined by 2.35 percent a year and thus helped moderate inflationary forces on net balance. In contrast, the unit fixed capital charges rose at an average annual rate of 5.4 percent in the first subperiod, accelerating to 6.9 percent in the second, contributing 18 percent of the inflation

Table 4-3. U.S. nonfinancial corporate business sector, components of price change, 1948-66 and 1966-76

| | 1948-66 | | | 1966-76 | | | |
| | Average annual percentage rate of change | Contribution to price change | | 1966 relative weights[d] (percentages) | Average annual percentage rate of change | Contribution to price change | |
		Percentage points[d]	Percent			Percentage points	Percent
Implicit price deflator	1.69	1.69	100.0	100.0	5.31	5.31	100.0
Unit indirect business taxes	2.38	0.21	12.4	10.1	5.32	0.53	10.2
Unit factor cost[a]	1.62	1.48	87.6	90.0	5.30	4.77	89.8
Average factor price	4.32	3.94			6.70	6.03	
Total factor productivity	2.65	-2.42			1.32	-1.19	
Unit labor costs	1.65	1.05	62.7	63.5	5.66	3.59	67.7
Average hourly compensation	4.80	3.07			7.57	4.81	
Real product per hour	3.10	-1.98			1.82	-1.16	
Unit capital costs[a]	1.52	0.42	24.9	26.5	4.43	1.17	22.1
Average price of capital	2.93	0.80			4.42	1.17	
Real product per unit of capital	1.35	-0.37			0.02	-0.01	
Unit fixed capital costs	5.43			10.9	6.87		
Unit depreciation[b]	5.14			9.2	5.55		
Unit net interest	7.21			1.7	12.13		
Unit profits[c]	-0.10			15.6	2.35		

[a]Includes unit profits.
[b]Without adjustment of capital consumption to replacement cost valuation (CCA).
[c]With inventory valuation adjustment (IVA), but without CCA.
[d]The 1948 relative weights are shown in Table 4-2.

rate during 1948-66 and 14 percent in the subsequent decade. Although net interest is a much smaller fraction of total cost than depreciation, its increase per unit of real product was much greater, particularly in the second subperiod. When the CCA is used in the computations, unit depreciation rises at a slower pace in the first subperiod and a faster pace in the second. Conversely, unit profits rose slightly instead of sagging in the first subperiod, but fell more sharply in the decade 1966-76 than did book profits per unit adjusted only for inventory valuation.

Components of the Price of Capital.   The two major components of the average price of capital are the price index for capital goods and the gross rate of return on the gross capital stock at replacement cost. This is evident when it is recalled that the average price of capital is obtained as the quotient of the gross income from capital and the real gross stock of capital. Gross income is the gross rate of return (r) times the current dollar gross stock of capital computed as the real gross stock (K_G^*) times the price deflator for capital goods (P_K). Thus: $rK_G^* P_K / K_G^* = rP_K$.

Looking at the periods under study, the price deflator for the gross capital stock rose by an average of 3.7 percent a year over the entire twenty-eight year period—2.1 percent in the 1948-66 subperiod and 6.5 percent in the following decade—somewhat more than the increase in the implicit price deflator for gross product. On the other hand, the gross rate of return with CCA declined by about 0.2 percent a year on average over the period as a whole, rising by an average 0.9 percent in the first eighteen years and then declining at an average annual rate of around 2 percent in the final decade. The sum of the rates of change in the two components approximately equals the product of the rates of change plus 100.0, which, in turn, equals the rate of change in the average price of capital shown in Tables 4-2 and 4-3 above.

Since the gross return consists of capital consumption, net interest paid, and profits before tax, it is of interest to see what happened to these returns as percentages of appropriate bases (Table 4-4). The calculated rate of depreciation on the gross capital stock, with both expressed at replacement costs, rose from 3.5 percent in 1948 to 4.4 percent in 1966 and to 5.2 percent in 1976 (line 15B). This increase largely reflects a shift in the composition of the stock toward shorter-lived fixed assets on which depreciation rates are higher.

Net interest paid on net liabilities (line 10) rose from 1.2 percent in 1948, to 3.1 percent in 1966, to 6.3 percent in 1976. These figures reflect differences in average rates received on financial assets and rates paid on total liabilities. But the trend reflects the upward trend in interest rates over the

Table 4-4. *U.S. nonfinancial corporate business sector,*
stock-flow relationships, 1948, 1966, and 1976
(billions of current dollars,* and percentage rates)

Line no.		1948	1966	1976
1.	Gross capital stock	302.7	804.0	2,064.6
2.	Net capital stock	154.4	450.2	1,156.2
3.	Financial assets	26.2	149.3	459.1
4.	Total assets (2+3)	180.5	599.5	1,615.3
5.	Liabilities	102.5	384.8	974.0
6.	Net liabilities (5−3)	76.3	235.5	514.9
7.	Net worth (4−5)	78.1	214.7	641.3
8A.	Profits before tax, w. IVA, w/o CCA	29.7	67.4	116.4
8B.	Profits before tax, w. IVA and CCA	25.8	71.2	101.9
9A.	Rate of return (w/o CCA) on net worth (8A + 7)	38.0	31.4	18.2
9B.	Rate of return (w. CCA) on net worth (8B + 7)	33.0	33.2	15.9
10.	Net interest paid	0.9	7.4	32.4
11.	Average net interest rate	1.2	3.1	6.3
12A.	Net capital return (w/o CCA) before tax (8A + 10)	30.6	74.8	148.8
12B.	Net capital return (w. CCA) before tax (8B + 10)	26.7	78.6	134.3
13A.	Net rate of return (w/o CCA) on capital (12A + 2)	19.8	16.6	12.9
13B.	Net rate of return (w. CCA) on capital (12B + 2)	17.3	17.5	11.6
14A.	Capital consumption allowances (w/o CCA)	6.8	39.5	92.5
14B.	Capital consumption allowances (w. CCA)	10.7	35.7	107.0
15A.	Rate of capital consumption (w/o CCA) (14A + 1)	2.3	4.9	4.5
15B.	Rate of capital consumption (w. CCA) (14B + 1)	3.5	4.4	5.2
16.	Gross capital return (12 + 14)	37.4	114.3	241.3
17.	Gross rate of return (16 + 2)	12.4	14.2	11.7
18.	Implicit price deflator for gross capital	53.5	78.0	146.2
19.	Average gross price of capital (17 $\times$ 18)	6.6	11.1	17.1

* = Fixed assets are valued at replacement cost.
IVA = inventory valuation adjustment.
CCA = capital consumption adjustment.

period, as influenced by the acceleration in actual and anticipated inflation rates.

When net interest is combined with profit before tax (after adjustment for inventory and capital consumption valuation), the net rate of return on capital (line 12) held slightly over 17 percent in both 1948 and 1966, and then dropped to 11.6 percent in 1976. Of particular interest is the rate of return on net worth (line 8). This rate is calculated at around 33 percent in both 1948 and 1966, before dropping drastically to 15.9 percent in 1976. It is apparent that macroeconomic policies designed to restrain inflation kept the increase in average prices below the increase in unit costs (exclusive of profits) on balance over the 1966-76 decade, resulting in a profit squeeze. This, in turn, was undoubtedly one of the factors accounting for the sluggish performance of business outlays for new plant and equipment during the recovery that began in 1976.

Industry Trends in Productivity, Factor Prices, Unit Costs, and Product Prices

It would be possible to analyze the rates of change in product prices for each of the thirty-one industry groups for which we present estimates in the same manner that we have done for the nonfinancial corporate sector. That is, we could show the extent to which changes in productivity have offset changes in factor prices, in total and for labor and capital separately, and have thus mitigated the effect of increasing factor prices on unit costs and product prices. But to do so for each industry would be of little general interest. Readers interested in particular industries can trace the interrelationships from the following tables. Instead, we analyze the interrelations for the array of industries as a whole to see what kind of generalizations can be made.

The basic hypothesis used to guide our inquiry is derived from *a priori* reasoning buttressed by the findings of earlier studies. It rests on the assumption that relative changes in factor prices are not usually correlated significantly with relative changes in productivity. Given a fair degree of mobility of resources among industries, it would be expected that over longer periods of time, factor prices would tend to show much the same rates of change in different industries. Certainly, if wage rates are tied to productivity change on an industry basis, the structure of wages would eventually be thrown out of alignment, given the different rates of productivity change in different industries. The same is true of the price of capital and its components: interest and profit rates, and the replacement costs (prices) of the underlying physical capital goods. Given a reasonable degree of competition, if factor prices in one industry tended to rise significantly more than average, there would be a tendency for resources to move into that industry, dampening the increases while raising the rates of increase in the industries out of which they were moving. This equalizing tendency should be more pronounced over longer periods than over fewer years, of course.

If this is the case, then there should be a negative correlation between relative industry changes in productivity and in unit costs and prices. That is, industries with above average productivity increases would have below average increases in unit costs (including profits). Unless relative price changes by industry were seriously distorted by differential movements in unit indirect business taxes, etc., the relative price changes should also show a significant negative correlation with relative changes in productivity.

To carry the argument a step further, if there is a reasonable degree of sensitivity of sales and output of the products of various industries to relative price change (not offset by a differential impact of income growth on demand, or by shifts in consumer preferences), one would expect a negative correlation between relative changes in prices and in output. To the extent that this is the case and/or there are differing opportunities for economies of scale related to rates of output growth, there should be a significant positive degree of correlation between relative changes in productivity and in output. If the relationship is strong enough, employment of labor and non-human resources should not be adversely affected by above average productivity gains.

In the following sections, we present the results of tests of the hypotheses just described, first with respect to TFP and unit costs, then for the labor and capital components. If the relationships hold for the totals, as they do in varying degree, they would also be expected to hold for the labor variables, in view of the preponderant weight of labor in total factor productivity and total factor costs. The relationships for the capital variables, not heretofore tested, would be less certain, however.

The correlations used in the analysis have been carried out for rates of change between 1948 and 1976, and for the 1948-66 and 1966-76 subperiods. This is the first time the relationships have been tested for the latter decade. Unfortunately, the terminal year of 1976 was not a cycle peak, high-employment year, and rates of change in relative profit rates, in particular, may be affected. Nevertheless, a decade is a long enough timespan for the basic relations to become apparent.

Total Factor Productivity, Costs, and Prices.   The annual industry product price indexes, changes in which are used in the correlations, are not product price indexes in the usual sense, but are the implicit price indexes for gross product originating in the various industries as estimated by the U.S. Department of Commerce. As noted earlier, industry gross product is the value of output less the cost of intermediate products consumed in production. The values of output and of intermediate product are separately deflated by corresponding price indexes and real industry product is the difference. The implicit deflator is obtained by dividing real product obtained by this "double-deflation" technique back into current dollar industry product. If output prices rise by more than intermediate goods prices, the implicit product deflator will rise by more than the output price index, and vice versa—the difference depending on the relative magnitude of intermediate purchases, as well as on the differential price trends for outputs and intermediate goods. For the business economy as a whole, the two sets of prices show much the same trends, since intermediate goods are a significant portion of output; for individual industries, there may be some divergence. But it is the implicit product deflator whose changes are most closely related to changes in unit factor costs, although it is the industry output prices whose relative changes should be more closely related to relative changes in sales and output.

As shown in Table 4-5 below, the rates of change in the product deflator are generally quite close to those in unit factor costs. The differences reflect differences between rates of change in unit factor cost and in indirect business taxes less subsidies, weighted by the ratio of the tax variable to gross product originating in each industry in the initial year. If unit indirect taxes, etc., rise by more than unit factor costs, which is generally the case, the product price deflator rises by more than unit factor costs, and vice versa. But since indirect business taxes less subsidies are generally less than 10 percent of gross product, the discrepancies between the unit cost and the product price changes are usually small. This is indicated by the high correlation coefficient between the relative rates of change in product prices and unit costs.

Before looking at the relationship between productivity and product prices, we must first establish the relationship between productivity and factor prices. As indicated in the matrix of correlation coefficients below (Table 4-6A), although there is a mildly positive degree of correlation between rates of change in TFP and in average factor prices, it is not significant at the 0.05 level. This is the case whether or not profit rates are included in factor prices.

Thus, it is not surprising, based on the reasoning of the previous section, that there is a significant negative correlation between relative changes in TFP and in unit costs or in product prices, as shown in the scatter diagram (Fig. 4-1). The fact that the correlation coefficients are practically the same, using changes in either unit factor costs or product prices correlated against TFP changes, reflects the fact that there is no systematic relationship between changes in indirect business taxes less subsidies and unit factor costs, as well as the comparatively small size of the tax element in product price changes for most industries. It is relevant to the above analysis that there is much greater variability in rates of change in TFP than in the rate of change in factor prices. It follows that the variability in rates of change in unit costs and in product prices is greater than in factor prices.

Table 4-5. *Components of changes in unit factor costs and product prices in the U.S. business economy, by major industry*

Part A. Average annual percentage rates of change, 1948-76

	Implicit product price deflator	Unit factor cost	Average factor price	Total factor productivity
Farming	1.7	1.6	4.7	3.0
Manufacturing	2.8	2.9	5.0	2.1
Food	2.2	2.6	5.5	2.9
Tobacco	1.8	4.7	7.3	2.6
Textiles	0.1	0.1	3.1	3.1
Apparel	1.5	1.5	4.0	2.5
Lumber	2.9	3.0	6.0	2.9
Furniture	2.9	2.8	4.7	1.8
Paper	2.9	2.8	4.9	2.0
Printing and publishing	3.5	3.5	5.1	1.5
Chemical	1.5	1.4	4.6	3.2
Petroleum	1.6	0.5	2.5	2.1
Rubber	2.9	3.2	5.0	1.8
Leather	2.9	2.8	4.0	1.1
Stone, clay and glass	3.7	3.7	5.0	1.3
Primary metals	5.2	5.1	5.2	0.1
Fabricated metals	3.6	3.8	5.3	1.3
Machinery, excluding electrical	3.8	3.8	4.9	1.7
Electrical machinery	1.2	1.3	5.1	3.7
Transportation equipment	2.5	2.7	5.5	2.7
Instruments	2.8	3.3	6.7	2.2
Miscellaneous manufactures	2.0	2.0	4.7	2.7
Nonfarm-nonmanufacturing	3.3	3.2	5.2	2.0
Mining	3.7	3.5	5.2	1.7
Construction	4.2	4.2	5.3	1.0
Total transportation	3.0	3.0	5.5	2.4
Railroad	2.2	2.4	4.9	2.5
Nonrail	3.9	3.8	5.4	1.6

	Implicit product price deflator	Unit factor cost	Average factor price	Total factor productivity
Communications	2.0	2.3	6.7	4.2
Public utilities	2.5	2.5	5.6	3.0
Trade	2.9	2.6	4.7	2.1
Finance and insurance	4.7	4.5	4.7	0.1
Real estate	3.2	3.0	5.9	2.8
Services	4.4	4.4	6.1	1.6
Business economy, total	3.0	2.9	5.3	2.3

Part B. Average annual percentage rates of change, 1948-66 and 1966-76

	Implicit product price deflator		Unit factor cost		Average factor price		Total factor productivity	
	1948-66	1966-76	1948-66	1966-76	1948-66	1966-76	1948-66	1966-76
Farming	-0.7	2.9	-0.9	6.2	2.6	8.6	3.5	2.2
Manufacturing	1.8	4.5	1.9	4.7	4.4	6.1	2.5	1.4
Food	1.3	4.0	1.4	4.8	4.4	7.5	3.0	2.6
Tobacco	1.4	2.6	3.6	6.7	6.2	9.5	2.5	2.6
Textiles	-1.8	3.6	-1.8	3.5	2.2	4.9	4.0	1.3
Apparel	0.8	2.8	0.8	2.7	2.9	6.0	2.1	3.2
Lumber	2.3	4.1	0.7	7.4	4.7	8.4	4.0	0.9
Furniture	2.3	4.1	2.3	3.8	4.5	5.1	2.1	1.3
Paper	1.8	5.0	1.7	4.9	3.9	6.8	2.2	1.8
Printing and publishing	2.2	6.0	2.2	5.9	4.6	6.0	2.4	-0-
Chemicals	0.5	3.3	0.4	3.3	4.0	5.8	3.5	2.5
Petroleum	0.7	3.4	-2.1	5.4	0.7	6.0	2.9	0.6
Rubber	1.9	4.6	2.0	5.3	4.2	6.5	2.2	1.1
Leather	2.2	4.2	2.2	4.1	3.3	5.2	1.1	1.1
Stone, clay and glass	2.4	6.1	2.4	6.1	4.1	6.8	1.7	0.6
Primary metals	4.1	7.4	4.0	7.0	5.0	5.5	1.0	-1.4
Fabricated metals	2.2	6.1	2.1	6.8	3.8	7.3	1.7	0.5
Machinery, excluding electrical	3.2	5.0	3.2	5.0	4.5	5.7	1.3	0.7
Electrical machinery	0.2	3.2	0.5	2.9	4.7	5.8	4.2	2.8
Transportation equipment	2.2	3.1	2.3	3.5	5.5	5.4	3.2	1.8
Instruments	2.6	3.2	3.0	4.1	6.1	5.0	3.1	0.8
Miscellaneous manufactures	1.0	3.9	1.0	3.8	3.9	6.4	2.8	2.5

Table 4-5. *Components of changes in unit factor costs and product prices in the U.S. business economy, by major industry*

Part B. Average annual percentage rates of change, 1948-66 and 1966-76 (cont.)

Nonfarm-nonmanufacturing	2.0	5.7	1.9	5.6	4.4	6.7	2.5	1.1
Mining	0.3	10.1	-0-	10.2	3.2	8.9	3.3	-1.2
Contract construction	1.9	8.4	1.8	8.6	4.4	6.8	2.5	-1.6
Total transportation	1.8	5.3	1.8	5.2	4.7	6.8	2.9	1.6
Railroad	-0-	6.2	0.4	6.1	4.6	5.4	4.2	-0.6
Nonrail	3.2	5.1	3.1	4.9	4.8	7.1	1.6	2.1
Communications	1.7	2.5	2.2	2.5	7.1	6.0	4.7	3.3
Public utilities	0.9	5.5	1.0	5.2	6.0	4.9	4.9	-0.3
Trade	1.3	5.9	0.9	5.7	3.4	7.2	2.5	1.4
Finance and insurance	4.5	5.2	4.4	4.8	4.8	4.4	0.4	-0.4
Real estate	2.6	4.3	2.3	4.3	5.7	6.2	3.4	1.8
Services	3.6	5.7	3.8	5.6	5.3	7.5	1.5	1.8
Private domestic business	1.7	5.3	1.6	5.3	4.6	6.7	2.9	1.4

Table 4-6. Matrix of correlation coefficients: rates of change in total factor productivity and in product prices vs. rates of change in associated variables, 1948-76, 1948-66, and 1966-76

Part A. 30 U.S. industry groups

	Average factor price	Unit factor cost Including profits	Unit factor cost Excluding profits	Average product price	Output (real product)	Total factor input	Persons engaged
Total factor productivity							
1948-76	.179	-.674b	-.710b	-.809b	.475b	-.075	-.156
1948-66	.141	-.609b	-.752b	-.688b	.335a	-.243	-.310
1966-76	.167	-.690b	-.737b	-.773b	.622b	-.047	-.069
Average product price							
1948-76	.289	.871b	.863b		-.206	.262	.365a
1948-66	.479b	.880b	.889b		-.076	.460b	.551b
1966-76	213	.789b	.670b		-.481b	.036	.115

Part B. 20 U.S. manufacturing industry groups

	Average factor price	Unit factor cost Including profits	Unit factor cost Excluding profits	Average product price	Output (real product)	Total factor input	Persons engaged
Total factor productivity							
1948-76	.051	-.650b	-.756b	-.849b	.601b	.049	-.035
1948-66	-.023	-.620b	-.789b	-.680b	.458a	-.024	-.032
1966-76	.240	-.611b	-.656b	-.799b	.649b		
Average product price							
1948-76	.326	.832b	.840b		-.405a	.088	.158
1948-66	.516a	.814b	.892b		-.158	.166	.236
1966-76	-.125	.549b	.536b		-.603b	-.005	.040

aSignificant at the .05 level.
bSignificant at the .01 level.

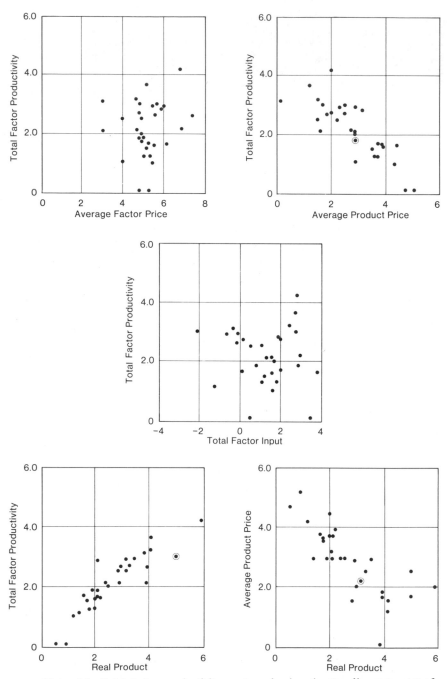

Figure 4-1. Total factor productivity, costs and prices (scatter diagrams, rates of change), 31 industries, 1948-76

Sources: U.S. Department of Labor; U.S. Department of Commerce; Conference Board.

Although industry price deflators are not perfect proxies for output prices, their relative changes are negatively correlated with relative changes in industry real product. In some of the industries that do not conform to this relationship, presumably the price elasticities of demand are low and/or outweighted by high income elasticities, or there are inadequacies of the real product estimates, as in the services sector.

Given the negative relationships both between relative changes in TFP and in product prices, and between relative changes in product prices and in real product, it would follow that there would be a positive relationship between relative changes in TFP and in real product. As shown in the table of correlation coefficients, the relation is positive and is significant at the 0.01 level. In fact, the correlation is stronger than would be expected based on the price linkage alone. This suggests that there is a reciprocal relationship of changes in output operating on changes in TFP through economies of scale.

If changes in output and in productivity were not positively correlated, then there would be a negative correlation between relative changes in productivity and in the employment of factors. Actually, the positive relationship between changes in TFP and output is strong enough to eliminate any systematic tendency for relative increases in productivity to be associated with relative declines in factor input. Although the latter two variables are negatively correlated, the coefficient is not significant at the 0.05 level. The relationships have more meaning when carried out in terms of the labor and capital factors separately, however, as is done in the following sections.

It may be helpful to trace through the relationships just established concretely for two of the thirty industries: first, communications, which had the highest rate of growth in TFP in 1948-76; then primary metals, which had the lowest growth of TFP among the manufacturing groups. Communications, consisting primarily of the telephone industry, increased TFP at an average annual rate of 4.2 percent during 1948-76. This offset about two-thirds of the mean increase in factor prices, which was above average, 6.7 percent a year, due to the heavy weight of capital in factor cost. The 2.3 percent a year increase in unit factor costs was associated with a 2 percent average annual increase in the product price deflator because of indirect business taxes, which, while above average as a percent of industry gross product in 1948, rose significantly less relative to output than did indirect business taxes in the business economy as a whole. The product price increase was the eighth lowest of the thirty industries, and well below the 2.8 percent average for all. Reflecting the relative price decline in part, and a strong income elasticity of demand as well, real product rose by 7.1 percent a year, on average, second only to electrical machinery and equipment (which had the second highest rate of productivity advance). Despite its high productivity growth, the communications industry raised its employment of factors by 3.8 percent a year, far above the 1.2 percent average annual increase in the business economy as a whole.

Primary metals, dominated by the steel industry, increased its TFP by only 0.1 percent a year during 1948-76. This provided a minimal offset to the industry's 5.2 percent a year average increase in factor prices, which was close to the economy average. The 5.1 percent a year average increase in unit factor cost was slightly under the 5.25 percent average increase in prices, since unit indirect business taxes had risen by more than the industry's unit costs. The price rise was the highest of the thirty industries and undoubtedly contributed to the relatively poor sales and output performance of primary metals, particularly in the face of better productivity and price performance of foreign competitors. The output growth of 1.56 percent a year was the second lowest of the twenty manufacturing industries, only exceeding that of leather and leather products (primarily shoes), which was also a low productivity performer. The increase of factor inputs into primary metals averaged 1.5 percent a year, only slightly above the business economy average, despite the sharp relative increase in its unit factor requirements.

The findings of this section make it clear that the firms with superior productivity performance benefit from the associated relative decline in price that is usually associated with relative increases in sales and output. Furthermore, the expansion of employment of labor and capital by the progressive industries is not adversely affected when the positive output effects of above average productivity advance offsets the input-conserving effects. The economics of each industry are unique, of course. But the estimates of productivity, costs, and prices are an essential starting point for the understanding of each.

Finally, going beyond industry statistics, it can be stated that relative levels and rates of change in productivity are basic to the profit performance of firms. Assuming firms operating in the same industry purchase their inputs and sell their outputs at comparable prices, then it is obvious that the lower the inputs per unit of output (or, the higher the productivity), the wider are the profit margins. Likewise, if productivity rises and unit costs drop relative to competitors, relative profit margins will rise. The competition among firms to maintain or improve profit margins is, of course, a major force behind productivity advance. It appears that an increasing number of firms are finding it useful to explicitly track their productivity performance not only for comparison purposes but also as a management tool to promote better productivity and as background for projections of output and input requirements.

Table 4-7. Components of changes in unit labor costs of the
U.S. business economy, by major industry group

| | Part A. Average annual percentage rates of change, 1948-76 | | |
	Unit labor cost	Average hourly compensation	Real product per hour
Farming	0.5	5.6	5.0
Manufacturing	3.0	5.7	2.6
Food	2.5	5.8	3.2
Tobacco	3.5	7.5	3.9
Textiles	1.6	4.4	2.8
Apparel	0.8	4.6	3.8
Lumber	2.7	6.3	3.5
Furniture	2.7	4.7	1.9
Paper	3.3	5.9	2.5
Printing and publishing	3.3	5.2	1.8
Chemicals	1.7	5.8	4.1
Petroleum	1.7	5.7	3.9
Rubber	3.3	5.3	2.1
Leather	3.2	4.5	1.4
Stone, clay, and glass	3.8	5.9	2.0
Primary metals	5.3	6.2	0.9
Fabricated metals	3.9	5.8	1.8
Machinery, excluding electrical	3.9	5.6	1.7
Electrical machinery	1.2	5.3	4.1
Transportation equipment	2.8	6.1	3.3
Instruments	3.1	6.2	2.9
Miscellaneous manufactures	2.2	5.3	3.0
Nonfarm-nonmanufacturing	3.1	5.6	2.4
Mining	3.4	5.6	2.1
Contract construction	4.2	5.4	1.2
Total transportation	3.2	5.9	2.6
Railroad	3.0	6.2	3.2
Nonrail	3.7	6.0	2.2
Communications	1.3	7.3	5.9
Public utilities	1.5	6.6	5.0
Trade	2.7	5.2	2.4
Finance and insurance	5.2	5.7	0.5
Real estate	1.3	3.4	2.1
Services	4.7	6.8	2.0
Private domestic business	2.9	5.9	3.0

Labor Productivity and Related Variables. Turning to the partial productivity ratios, (Table 4-7) note first that industry changes in real product per labor hour are highly correlated with changes in TFP (Table 4-8A). This is to be expected, since labor is the predominant factor input. More surprising is the fact that relative changes in labor productivity and in real product per unit of capital input show a significant positive correlation. In other words, industries with above average productivity gains tend to conserve more on both labor and capital inputs per unit of output, and vice versa. Earlier

*Table 4-7. Components of changes in unit labor costs of the
U.S. business economy, by major industry group*

Part B. Average annual percentage rates of change,
1948-66 and 1966-76

	Unit labor cost		Average hourly compensation		Real product per hour	
	1948-66	1966-76	1948-66	1966-76	1948-66	1966-76
Farming	−0.8	3.0	4.5	7.6	5.4	4.5
Manufacturing	1.8	5.1	4.8	7.4	2.9	2.2
Food	1.6	4.2	5.0	7.3	3.3	3.0
Tobacco	2.7	4.8	6.8	8.9	4.0	3.9
Textiles	−1.4	4.8	3.6	6.5	5.0	1.7
Apparel	0.9	2.9	3.1	6.8	2.2	3.9
Lumber	0.7	6.4	4.7	9.3	3.9	2.8
Furniture	2.0	4.1	4.0	5.8	2.0	1.6
Paper	2.2	5.1	4.7	7.9	2.4	2.7
Printing and publishing	1.9	6.0	4.4	6.7	2.4	0.7
Chemicals	0.6	3.6	5.1	7.0	4.5	3.3
Petroleum	−0.3	5.3	4.8	7.2	5.1	1.9
Rubber	1.9	5.7	4.2	7.4	2.3	1.6
Leather	2.5	4.4	3.7	6.2	1.2	1.7
Stone, clay, and glass	2.4	6.4	4.8	7.8	2.4	1.3
Primary metals	3.5	8.6	5.2	8.1	1.7	−0.5
Fabricated metals	2.1	7.2	4.3	8.4	2.2	1.2
Machinery, excluding electrical	2.9	5.7	4.6	7.4	1.7	1.7
Electrical machinery	0.1	3.0	4.4	7.0	4.3	3.8
Transportation equipment	2.1	4.0	5.6	7.2	3.4	3.0
Instruments	1.5	6.1	5.1	8.0	3.6	1.8
Miscellaneous manufactures	1.4	3.7	4.3	7.0	2.9	3.2
Nonfarm-nonmanufacturing	1.6	5.9	4.7	7.4	3.0	1.4
Mining	−0.1	10.0	4.2	8.1	4.2	−1.7
Contract construction	2.0	8.4	4.7	6.8	2.7	−1.5
Total transportation	1.5	6.1	4.9	7.7	3.3	1.5
Railroad	−0−	8.6	4.9	8.6	4.9	0.1
Nonrail	2.8	5.4	5.1	7.6	2.3	2.1
Communications	−0−	3.7	6.5	8.7	6.4	4.9
Public utilities	−0.9	5.8	5.9	7.9	6.8	2.0
Trade	1.4	5.1	4.3	6.7	2.8	1.6
Finance and insurance	4.5	6.5	5.4	6.2	0.9	−0.2
Real estate	−0.5	4.6	2.7	4.7	3.3	−0−
Services	3.3	7.2	5.3	9.6	1.9	2.3
Private domestic business	1.5	5.4	5.1	7.5	3.5	2.0

studies show that this higher efficiency also carries over to the use of materials and other intermediate products per unit of output.[1]

There is a mild positive correlation between relative industry changes in real product per hour and compensation per hour, significant at the 0.05 level

[1] See John W. Kendrick, *Productivity Trends in the United States* (New York: National Bureau of Economic Research, 1961), Table 56, p. 200.

for the period 1948-76 and the 1948-66 subperiod, but not for the 1966-76 subperiod. This was also true for eighty manufacturing industries during the previous half-century.[2]

Despite this mild degree of positive association between relative changes in productivity and in average hourly earnings, there is a highly significant negative correlation between relative changes in real product per hour and in unit labor costs and in product prices. As would be expected, the negative correlation is somewhat higher between changes in labor productivity and in unit labor costs than between the former and price changes, since unit labor cost is only one component of price, albeit the major component. As shown in Table 4-9A, the negative correlation between changes in labor productivity and in prices is higher for the entire period than for the subperiods, and higher for 1966-76 than for the earlier subperiod.

Given the negative correlation between relative industry changes in product prices and in output shown in Table 4-6A, changes in real product per hour are positively correlated with changes in real product (output). The coefficients of correlation are not as high as those between changes in TFP and in output, however, although the coefficient for the 1948-76 period is significant at the 0.05 level and that for the 1966-76 subperiod is significant at the 0.01 level.

The positive association between industry changes in productivity and in output was not strong enough to prevent a mild, but significant, negative correlation between changes in real product per hour and in labor input, whether measured by hours or by persons engaged in production (Table 4-8A).[3] This, of course, is one of the reasons for interindustry shifts of labor. Outside of farming and mining, however, there are few major industry groups in which employment has declined absolutely. And there is no reason why relative employment declines in some industries should be associated with increases in the economy-wide unemployment rate, given appropriate macroeconomic policies to sustain a rate of aggregate economic growth commensurate with the growth of the labor force and of productivity.

This is not to say that the cost-reducing technological changes underlying productivity advance are not a major factor in labor displacement from particular occupations and industries, and thus contribute to the frictional unemployment that is a normal feature of a dynamic economy. But mainten-

[2] Ibid., Table 55, p. 198.

[3] This differs from findings for the earlier half-century, over which the positive coefficients of correlation between changes in productivity and in output were higher; and the correlation between changes in productivity and in employment was positive, although not in all subperiods. See Kendrick, ibid., Table 63, p. 216.

Table 4-8. *Matrix of correlation coefficients: rates of change in real product per labor hour vs. rates of change in associated variables, 1948-76, 1948-66, and 1966-76.*

Part A. 30 U.S. industry groups

	Average hourly compensation	Unit labor cost	Average product price	Output (real product)	Labor input	Output per unit		Capital per unit of labor input	Persons engaged
						Total factor input	Capital input		
Output per hour									
1948-76	.362[a]	-.789[b]	-.766[b]	.397[a]	-3.19[a]	.898[b]	.554[b]	.428[b]	-.301[a]
1948-66	.308	-.836[b]	-.682[b]	.253	-.447[a]	.919[b]	.341	.489[b]	-.426[a]
1966-76	.222	-.821[b]	-.748[b]	.527[b]	-.309[a]	.884[b]	.500[b]	.512[b]	-.266

Part B. 20 U.S. manufacturing industry groups

	Average hourly compensation	Unit labor cost	Average product price	Output (real product)	Output per unit		Per unit of labor input		Persons engaged
					Total factor input	Capital input			
Output per hour									
1948-76	.244	-.766[b]	-.833[b]	.588[b]	-.085	.909[b]	.699[b]	.129	-.104
1948-66	.298	-.784[b]	-.695[b]	.344	-.217	.872[b]	.321	.415[a]	-.229
1966-76	.047	-.804[b]	-.802[b]	.679[b]	-.121	.950[b]	.667[b]	.149	-.161

[a]Indicates that coefficient of correlation is significant at the 0.05 level.
[b]Indicates significance at the 0.01 level.

ance of adequate aggregate demand and special programs designed to facilitate labor mobility, such as those provided for by the Comprehensive Employment and Training Act of 1973, as amended, help to minimize the human costs of technological progress.

Capital Productivity and Related Variables.   The coefficient of correlation between changes in capital productivity and in TFP (Tables 4-9 and 4-10) is higher than that between changes in the two partial productivity ratios— and is signficant at the 0.01 level. This is to be expected, since capital productivity is a component of TFP.

Even more so than in the case of labor, changes in real product per unit of capital input are positively correlated with changes in the price of capital, by industry. Despite this positive correlation, industry changes in capital productivity were negatively associated with changes in unit capital costs (exclusive of profits), and even more so with product prices. The coefficients of correlation between the productivity and price changes were significant over the period as a whole and in the 1966-76 subperiod. Consequently, there was a positive correlation between changes in capital productivity and in real product, with a lower coefficient for the 1948-66 subperiod and for the entire period.

As in the case of the corresponding labor variables, the correlation was not close enough to prevent a negative correlation between industry changes in capital productivity and in capital input. The coefficient was not significant for the subperiod 1966-76, however.

In conclusion, it is apparent that the hypothesized relationships are stronger when dealing with TFP and related variables than when dealing with the partial productivity ratios individually. That is, there is a smaller degree of correlation between changes in TFP and average factor prices than there is between changes in the partials and in their prices. Consequently, the negative correlation between changes in product prices and in productivity is higher for TFP than for the partials, and the same is true for the positive correlation between changes in productivity and in output. As a result, there is an insignificant negative correlation between relative changes in TFP and in total factor input, whereas the correlations are significantly negative (although still not large) between changes in each partial productivity ratio and the corresponding input. All this suggests a significant degree of substitutability between the factors over and above the basic complementarity. Further research on these matters is needed, although it lies outside the scope of this study.

Table 4-9. Components of changes in unit capital costs of the U.S. business economy, by major industry group

Part A. Average annual percentage rates of change, 1948-76

	Unit fixed capital costs	Unit profits	Average price of capital	Real product per unit of capital
Farming	7.63	0.19	7.29	-0.15
Manufacturing	6.79	0.81	7.33	0.34
Food	5.25	1.84	7.12	1.90
Tobacco	9.47	4.42	10.73	1.39
Textiles	4.99	-5.43	4.47	-0.42
Apparel	3.68	0.12	4.08	0.45
Lumber	7.13	2.60	9.35	1.99
Furniture	4.33	3.12	5.72	1.34
Paper	6.22	0.66	7.20	0.96
Printing and publishing	7.32	3.38	7.94	0.62
Chemicals	5.30	-0.51	7.16	1.76
Petroleum	7.45	n.a.	8.47	0.79
Rubber	5.02	1.60	5.83	0.71
Leather	7.14	-0.60	6.61	-0.69
Stone, clay and glass	7.73	0.89	6.91	-0.79
Primary metals	9.20	0.41	6.49	-2.36
Fabricated metals	6.61	2.21	5.18	-1.38
Machinery, excluding electrical	7.26	1.83	6.33	-0.96
Electrical machinery	6.64	0.11	8.78	1.90
Transportation equipment	8.09	0.32	9.38	0.97
Instruments	8.20	3.43	8.12	-0.08
Miscellaneous manufactures	4.48	-0.95	5.87	1.42
Mining	5.59	2.83	6.63	0.99
Construction	7.84	n.a.	5.33	-2.28
Total transportation	5.08	n.a.	6.81	1.41
Railroad	5.11	n.a.	4.00	-0.58
Nonrail	5.47	-2.45	4.78	-0.69

	Unit fixed capital costs	Unit profits	Average price of capital	Real product per unit of capital
Communications	5.52	2.74	6.86	1.29
Public utilities	5.39	-0.11	6.79	1.39
Trade	4.60	1.26	4.97	0.34
Finance and insurance	5.47	3.86	3.63	-1.76
Real estate	5.63	0.31	8.72	2.87
Services	6.36	2.23	6.11	-0.08
Nonfarm-nonmanufacturing	6.16	1.39	7.29	1.15
Private domestic business	6.37	0.98	7.39	1.06

Part B. Average annual percentage rates of change, 1948-66

	Unit fixed capital costs	Unit profits	Average price of capital	Real product per unit of capital
Farming	7.24	-5.47	6.29	-0.59
Manufacturing	6.04	0.93	7.49	1.03
Food	4.61	-0.61	6.70	2.18
Tobacco	3.42	4.48	4.24	1.16
Textiles	4.55	-4.30	3.78	-0.60
Apparel	3.68	-0.53	5.30	1.40
Lumber	5.11	0.30	9.89	4.39
Furniture	4.08	5.02	6.92	2.67
Paper	6.18	-0.82	7.70	1.45
Printing and publishing	5.82	2.88	8.15	2.30
Chemicals	4.28	-0.94	6.29	2.02
Petroleum	7.19	n.a.	8.72	1.26
Rubber	3.55	1.99	5.35	1.59
Leather	6.29	-0.62	7.06	0.45
Stone, clay and glass	7.74	0.05	7.21	-0.57
Primary metals	8.75	4.00	6.97	-1.46
Fabricated metals	5.09	1.40	4.09	-1.03
Machinery, excluding electrical	6.07	3.49	6.01	-0.27

Table 4-9. Components of changes in unit capital costs of the U.S. business economy, by major industry group

Part B. Average annual percentage rates of change, 1948-66 (cont.)

	Unit fixed capital costs	Unit profits	Average price of capital	Real product per unit of capital
Electrical machinery	4.55	1.40	8.27	3.36
Transportation equipment	8.83	1.34	11.68	2.26
Instruments	10.28	8.42	11.01	0.67
Miscellaneous manufactures	1.69	-1.67	4.08	2.54
Mining	4.35	-1.90	6.16	1.74
Construction	4.65	n.a.	2.79	-1.76
Total transportation	4.99	-1.18	6.61	1.18
Railroad	4.94	-3.19	4.61	0.27
Nonrail	5.45	2.28	3.46	-1.88
Communications	4.17	8.55	5.22	1.06
Public utilities	3.25	1.78	6.09	2.93
Trade	4.29	-4.10	4.39	0.18
Finance and insurance	4.33	4.12	2.67	-1.65
Real estate	5.21	0.28	8.85	3.40
Services	6.46	4.23	5.89	-0.22
Nonfarm-nonmanufacturing	5.57	0.61	7.06	1.51
Private domestic business	5.70	0.12	7.13	1.49

Part C. Average annual percentage rates of change, 1966-76

	Unit fixed capital costs	Unit profits	Average price of capital	Real product per unit of capital
Farming	8.35	11.22	9.10	0.65
Manufacturing	8.15	0.61	7.05	-0.89
Food	6.41	6.34	7.87	1.40
Tobacco	21.24	4.33	23.43	1.81
Textiles	5.79	-7.44	5.72	-0.08
Apparel	3.68	1.30	1.93	-1.25
Lumber	10.86	6.85	8.40	-2.18

Furniture	4.78	−0.23	3.61	−1.01
Paper	6.29	3.38	6.30	0.01
Printing and publishing	10.07	4.28	7.56	−2.33
Chemicals	7.18	0.29	8.73	1.29
Petroleum	7.94	−9.57	8.04	−0.04
Rubber	7.70	0.89	6.70	−0.84
Leather	8.67	−1.67	5.79	−2.71
Stone, clay and glass	7.71	2.41	6.39	−1.18
Primary metals	10.03	−5.75	5.63	−3.96
Fabricated metals	9.39	3.68	7.18	−1.99
Machinery, excluding electrical	9.43	−1.09	6.91	−2.18
Electrical machinery	10.50	−2.16	9.69	−0.69
Transportation equipment	6.76	−1.50	5.36	−1.29
Instruments	4.56	−4.98	3.09	−1.43
Miscellaneous manufactures	9.69	0.36	9.17	−0.55
Mining	7.86	11.92	7.49	−0.35
Construction	13.81	−31.53	10.07	−3.21
Total transportation	5.22	n.a.	7.18	1.82
Railroad	5.40	n.a.	2.92	−2.09
Nonrail	5.51	−10.40	7.18	1.50
Communication	7.99	−6.94	9.88	1.69
Public utilities	9.36	−3.41	8.07	−1.31
Trade	5.15	11.69	6.02	0.65
Finance and insurance	7.56	3.39	5.38	−1.97
Real estate	6.40	0.20	8.50	1.93
Services	6.20	−1.27	6.52	0.17
Nonfarm-nonmanufacturing	7.22	2.80	7.69	0.52
Private domestic business	7.59	2.54	7.86	0.29

Table 4-10. *Matrix of correlation coefficients: rates of change in real product per unit of capital vs. rates of change in associated variables, 1948-76, 1948-66, and 1966-76*

Part A. 30 U.S. industry groups

| | Price of capital | Unit capital cost | | | Average product price | Output (real product) | Capital input | Total factor productivity | Persons engaged |
		Incl. profit	Excl. profit	Unit profits					
Output per unit of capital input									
1948-76	.564b	.094	-.304	.111	-.530b	.459b	-.317	.747b	.055
1948-66	.569b	.080	-.281	-.005	-.257	.307	-.508b	.552b	.027
1966-76	.413a	.201	-.083	.246	-.427a	.680b	-.138	.700b	.292

a Indicates that coefficient of correlation is significant at the 0.05 level.
b Indicates significance at the 0.01 level.

Part B. 20 U.S. manufacturing industry groups

| | Price of capital | Excl. profits | Unit capital cost | | Average product price | Output (real product) | Capital input | Total factor productivity | Persons engaged |
			Excl. profits	Unit profits					
Output per unit of capital input									
1948-76	.434a	-.042	-.350a	.157	-.567b	.476a	-.346	.809b	.072
1948-66	.370	-.096	-.378a	-.059	-.206	.238	-.513a	.611b	.111
1966-76	.512a	.265	.154	.170	-.707b	.692b	-.373	.715b	.182

a Indicates that coefficient of correlation is significant at 0.05.
b Indicates that coefficient of correlation is significant at 0.01.

In comparing the present findings with those for earlier periods, it appears that the hypothesized relationships are less close for the period since 1948 than they were before World War II. This may reflect changes in the degree of competition in labor and product markets. But here again, further research is called for before explanations can be given. Nevertheless, the positive correlation between relative changes in productivity and in output remains significantly high and continues to help explain changes in the industrial structure of the economy.

CHAPTER 5

Cyclical Behavior of Productivity and Related Variables

Productivity plays a critical role in the economic developments that eventually lead to business downturns and subsequent recoveries of the economy, since cyclical movements of productivity are related to changes in costs, profits, output, and other key aspects of economic activity. The first part of this chapter discusses productivity changes over the postwar business cycles for the major sectors and the twenty manufacturing industries. In the second part, the discussion turns to the productivity-cost-price nexus over the cycle to further explore the role that productivity plays in modern economic fluctuations.

Productivity during Periods of Economic Expansion

Since total factor productivity (TFP) is measured as the ratio of output to (weighted) capital and labor, changes in any of these three elements will affect productivity. In particular, changes in the level of economic activity have an impact on productivity through variations in output, capacity utilization, and the quality of labor.

Tables 5-1 and 5-2 present rates of change in gross product originating and TFP as measured from quarterly reference cycle trough to peak dates over the postwar business cycles. As would be expected, during expansion periods output rises at rates higher than over long periods (Table 3-2). For example, the median rate of change in output for the private domestic busi-

*Table 5-1. Rates of growth during expansion periods, by major sector
(average annual percentage rates of change)*

Business reference cycles* (years and quarters)	Private domestic business economy	Farming	Nonfarm, nonmanufacturing	Manufacturing
Gross product originating				
1949-4 to 1953-3	6.4	1.1	5.2	9.8
1954-2 to 1957-3	4.4	0.6	4.9	4.0
1958-2 to 1960-2	5.8	1.0	5.1	8.3
1961-1 to 1969-4	4.7	−0.3	4.4	6.1
1970-4 to 1973-4	5.3	1.0	4.9	6.8
Median	5.3	1.0	4.9	6.8
Total factor productivity				
1949-4 to 1953-3	4.2	4.9	3.3	3.6
1954-2 to 1957-3	2.7	2.2	2.6	1.9
1958-2 to 1960-2	3.3	2.2	2.6	4.3
1961-1 to 1969-4	2.8	2.6	2.2	3.1
1970-4 to 1973-4	2.0	0.4	1.1	3.7
Median	2.8	2.2	2.6	3.6

*Based on National Bureau of Economic Research cyclical reference periods.
Source: The Conference Board.

ness economy is 5.3 percent, as compared to its long-term growth rate (1948-76) of 3.5 percent. Only the farm sector exhibits the same output growth during expansion periods as over the past twenty-eight years as a whole, since farm output is not very sensitive to changes in economic activity.

Total factor productivity of the major sectors, too, shows stronger growth during expansionary periods. One reason is the movement from low rates of utilization of capacity back toward more efficient utilization rates. Examination of the postwar expansion periods does not indicate any pattern toward slower, or faster, productivity growth. But for the overall economy the period of slowest growth in productivity was the most recent expansionary period (1970-4 to 1973-4).

Industries within the manufacturing sector show the same basic pattern as the major nonfarm sectors of high growth in output and productivity during business expansions. The median rate of change in output (Table 5-2) over the four most recent expansionary periods, covering 1954 through 1973, ranges from a low of 2.2 percent for the food industry to 12.6 percent for the rubber industry. Total factor productivity growth rates also vary quite considerably among the manufacturing industries, ranging from 0.6 to 6.5 percent for the nonelectrical machinery and chemical industries, respectively. The high correlation between output and productivity rates of change is apparent when comparing the median rates of change of the industries.

Table 5-2. Rates of growth during expansion periods, by manufacturing industry (average annual percentage rates of change)

	Business reference cycles*				
	1954-2 to 1957-3	1958-2 to 1960-2	1961-1 to 1969-4	1970-4 to 1973-4	Median
	Gross product originating				
Food	3.7	0.5	3.1	1.2	2.2
Tobacco	4.2	9.6	1.2	1.6	2.9
Textiles	4.3	8.3	7.4	3.5	5.8
Apparel	2.5	6.2	4.1	11.0	5.2
Lumber	3.5	12.7	6.1	5.4	5.8
Furniture	2.8	10.7	6.1	13.4	8.4
Paper	2.0	7.8	5.6	15.1	6.7
Printing and publishing	3.7	4.6	4.4	6.3	4.5
Chemicals	9.3	10.3	7.8	7.4	8.6
Petroleum	3.6	6.7	3.8	3.0	3.7
Rubber	0.8	15.1	10.1	15.9	12.6
Leather	3.3	7.2	1.8	4.2	3.8
Stone, clay and glass	3.8	8.3	3.9	9.4	6.1
Primary metals	7.1	2.5	6.3	11.3	6.7
Fabricated metals	3.4	5.0	6.5	11.3	5.8
Machinery, excluding electrical	−0.7	3.7	6.0	9.6	4.8
Electrical machinery	4.9	10.9	9.9	12.4	10.4
Transportation equipment	0.6	3.1	8.8	16.1	6.0
Instruments	0.8	7.4	8.5	11.4	8.0
Miscellaneous manufactures	4.7	7.5	4.6	7.6	6.1
	Total factor productivity				
Food	1.5	0.2	2.6	1.8	1.7
Tobacco	1.2	7.6	2.4	1.2	1.8
Textiles	4.3	4.1	5.5	0.9	4.2
Apparel	0.2	1.6	2.0	8.9	1.8
Lumber	6.8	8.8	4.3	-0-	5.6
Furniture	0.2	4.4	2.8	7.7	3.6
Paper	0.7	4.0	3.1	13.8	3.6
Printing and publishing	2.5	2.1	2.0	4.8	2.3
Chemicals	6.3	7.1	4.7	6.6	6.5
Petroleum	1.6	7.8	2.7	1.8	2.3
Rubber	−3.3	7.6	4.2	9.1	5.9
Leather	3.0	4.7	2.4	6.1	3.9
Stone, clay and glass	0.7	2.3	1.6	5.6	2.0
Primary metals	3.4	−3.8	3.1	7.9	3.3
Fabricated metals	0.2	0.1	2.5	6.1	1.4
Machinery, excluding electrical	−3.4	−0.7	1.8	4.4	0.6
Electrical machinery	1.2	1.5	5.6	7.9	3.1
Transportation equipment	−0.7	1.0	4.4	11.5	2.7
Instruments	−1.7	1.9	4.5	6.3	3.2
Miscellaneous manufactures	4.7	4.7	1.8	5.2	4.7

*Based on National Bureau of Economic Research cyclical reference periods.
Source: The Conference Board.

Table 5-3. Rates of growth during contraction periods, by major sector
(average annual percentage rates of change)

Business reference cycles* (years and quarters)	Private domestic business economy	Farming	Nonfarm, nonmanufacturing	Manufacturing
Gross product originating				
1948-4 to 1949-4	−3.4	−4.1	−2.0	−6.2
1953-3 to 1954-2	−4.1	−1.0	−0.2	−12.2
1957-3 to 1958-2	−5.5	5.9	−0.8	−17.9
1960-2 to 1961-1	−1.9	1.9	1.0	−9.3
1969-4 to 1970-4	−1.0	10.4	1.5	−8.0
1973-4 to 1975-1	−5.7	−3.7	−1.9	−15.0
Median	−3.8	0.5	−0.5	−10.8
Total factor productivity				
1948-4 to 1949-4	0.2	2.7	−1.2	1.4
1953-3 to 1954-2	−1.2	1.7	−0.4	−2.9
1957-3 to 1958-2	−0.3	12.8	1.7	−7.8
1960-2 to 1961-1	−0.5	1.0	0.8	−3.5
1969-4 to 1970-4	0.3	11.5	0.4	−1.7
1973-4 to 1975-1	−2.8	−2.1	−0.4	−8.9
Median	−0.4	2.2	0.2	−3.2

*Based on National Bureau of Economic Research cyclical reference periods.
Source: The Conference Board.

In contrast, the performance of productivity over contraction periods is poor, as would be expected, since during economic declines output falls faster than labor and capital inputs and capacity utilization rates drop. During the six postwar contraction periods (Table 5-3), output of the private domestic business economy declined at a median rate of 3.8 percent. However, the brunt of these recessions was borne by the manufacturing sector, which had a median rate of decline of output of 10.8 percent. For the most part, the other two sectors had relatively low rates of decline or even gains in their output, since the type of activities with which these two sectors are involved must be maintained (such as medical services) during economic downturns.

Changes in productivity during contraction periods show a picture similar to output rates of growth. The farm and nonfarm-nonmanufacturing sectors experienced gains in their productivity during most of the six recessions. In contrast, the manufacturing sector suffered strong declines in its productivity, except for the 1948-49 recession. Overall, the median decline in manufacturing productivity is 3.2 percent per annum. Here, too, the strong decline in output of this sector helps explain its loss of productivity during business contractions.

Table 5-4. Rates of growth during contraction periods, by manufacturing industry (average annual percentage rates of change)

| | Business reference cycles* | | | | |
	1957-3 to 1958-2	1960-2 to 1961-1	1969-4 to 1970-4	1973-4 to 1975-1	Median
	Gross product originating				
Food	1.1	2.8	4.3	−5.7	2.0
Tobacco	−9.0	0.6	10.7	−2.4	−0.9
Textiles	−6.0	−16.1	4.0	−22.2	−11.1
Apparel	−1.8	−9.4	−6.6	−15.0	−8.0
Lumber	−10.7	−22.4	5.1	−13.7	−12.2
Furniture	−5.8	−20.3	−26.0	−24.6	−22.5
Paper	3.3	−6.1	−19.4	−27.5	−12.8
Printing and publishing	−1.2	−1.0	−10.2	−11.8	−5.7
Chemicals	−4.7	−8.5	−2.6	−13.1	−6.6
Petroleum	4.5	−1.9	6.0	−3.6	2.0
Rubber	−4.8	−17.1	−26.0	−31.8	−21.6
Leather	−10.1	− 0.8	−10.5	−21.8	−5.5
Stone, clay and glass	1.2	−15.0	−10.0	−23.1	−12.5
Primary metals	−30.5	−42.0	−18.5	−17.1	−24.5
Fabricated metals	−2.5	−11.7	−20.9	−22.9	−16.3
Machinery, excluding electrical	−1.9	0.1	−7.5	−10.5	−4.7
Electrical machinery	−0.6	0.6	−14.8	−18.8	−7.7
Transportation equipment	−3.6	−31.9	−44.6	−28.5	−30.2
Instruments	9.4	−7.5	−27.5	−12.5	−10.0
Miscellaneous manufactures	−0.1	−11.7	−10.0	−11.5	−10.8
	Total factor productivity				
Food	12.8	5.3	5.1	−3.0	5.2
Tobacco	4.7	−7.6	8.7	−1.0	2.9
Textiles	2.9	−6.3	9.2	−5.4	−1.3
Apparel	9.4	−6.6	−2.6	−2.3	−3.0
Lumber	0.5	−5.8	8.2	−5.7	−2.6
Furniture	7.2	−8.7	−20.1	−6.9	−7.8
Paper	5.6	−4.5	−16.7	−22.6	−10.6
Printing and Publishing	−1.2	−2.3	−7.9	−10.7	−5.1
Chemicals	−6.3	−7.0	−2.0	−12.8	−6.7
Petroleum	5.3	0.4	2.7	−5.4	1.6
Rubber	11.4	−11.3	−20.2	−21.4	−15.8
Leather	4.5	−13.8	−4.6	−10.0	−7.8
Stone, clay, and glass	8.0	−3.1	−6.7	−14.9	−4.9
Primary metals	−12.1	−26.9	−9.4	−11.3	−16.7
Fabricated metals	11.4	−1.3	−12.8	−14.8	−7.1
Machinery, excluding electrical	11.6	10.3	0.1	−3.4	5.2
Electrical machinery	13.1	−0.5	−7.8	−10.6	−4.2
Transportation equipment	12.5	−24.4	−27.1	−19.4	−21.9
Instruments	16.4	−5.7	−22.7	−11.5	−8.6
Miscellaneous manufactures	8.1	−2.5	−6.4	−3.9	−3.2

*Based on National Bureau of Economic Research cyclical reference periods.
Source: The Conference Board.

Rates of change in output during contraction periods for the manufacturing industries (Table 5-4) give an idea as to the degree of cyclicality of each industry. Some industries, such as food, tobacco, and petroleum, have experienced either small declines or even gains in their output. Others are very cyclical, such as the transportation equipment, primary metals, furniture, and rubber industries, which have experienced median rates of decline in their output of over 20 percent.

The same pattern is true for TFP. Those industries that produce products that are necessities and not postponable, such as food, tobacco, and petroleum, experience gains in productivity during recessions. In contrast, the cyclically sensitive industries—those producing products the purchase of which may be postponed—have sharp declines in their productivity growth rates. One example is the transportation equipment industry, which produces cars and trucks. Output of this industry has been quite volatile, as has its productivity, which has declined at a median rate of 21.9 percent over the last five business slowdowns.

The measures of productivity growth rates during contraction periods presented here probably underestimate the impact of recessions on each industry's productivity, since the peaks and troughs used in the calculations are the general economy's reference dates rather than the industry's specific peak and trough dates with respect to productivity. Usually, productivity gains begin to taper off well before the economy hits a peak. Productivity also starts to revive again as the economy approaches the bottom of its cycle. Therefore, using the reference dates to measure rates of change of productivity is likely to lessen the measured changes in productivity during contractions. Clearly, however, there is quite a variability in the sensitivity of each sector and manufacturing industry to the business cycle, and the performance of a sector's/industry's productivity during both an economic expansion and contraction is closely tied to changes in its output.

The Productivity-Cost-Price Nexus over the Cycle

The systematic tendency for rates of change in productivity to lead business cycle turning points is an important part of the explanation of economic fluctuation, as first developed by Wesley C. Mitchell in 1913.[1] Briefly, Mitchell and subsequent investigators pointed out that the tendency for output per hour to drop, or its rate of increase to decelerate, before cycle peaks, in conjunction with continued increases in average hourly earnings, resulted in an acceleration of increases in unit labor costs, which at some point

[1]Wesley C. Mitchell, *Business Cycles* (Berkeley: University of California Press, 1913).

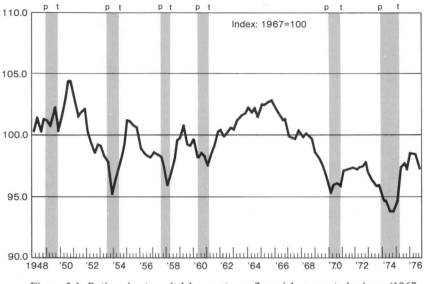

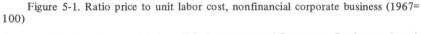

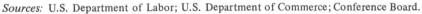

Figure 5-1. Ratio price to unit labor cost, nonfinancial corporate business (1967= 100)

Sources: U.S. Department of Labor; U.S. Department of Commerce; Conference Board.

exceeds that in prices, with a consequent drop in profit margins. In a profit-motivated enterprise system, the decline in profit margins reduces internal sources of funds, creates adverse expectations, and leads to a drop in new orders for equipment and in construction contract awards, thus playing a crucial role in turning aggregate business activity down. Conversely, the increase in labor productivity or in its rate of change before the trough, while average hourly earnings gains are still falling, reduces unit labor costs in relation to prices, widens profit margins, and sets the stage for recovery.

Subsequent investigators have determined that the sequence outlined by Mitchell has operated with surprising regularity in the period since World War II.[2] Instead of average earnings and prices actually declining in a recession, however, the declines have been confined to rates of change since the 1948-49 contraction. Nevertheless, the ratio of prices to unit labor costs has described a cycle in absolute terms, with a pronounced tendency to lead general business activity at both peaks and troughs, based on the reference cycle turning points established by the National Bureau of Economic Re-

[2] Anthony Clough, "Prices, Unit Labor Costs and Profits: An Examination of Wesley C. Mitchell's Business Cycle Theory for the Period 1947-1969," doctoral dissertation, George Washington University, Washington, D.C., June 1970; Geoffrey Moore, "Productivity, Costs and Prices: New Light from an Old Hypothesis," in National Bureau of Economic Research, *Explorations in Economic Research* (Winter 1975): 1-17.

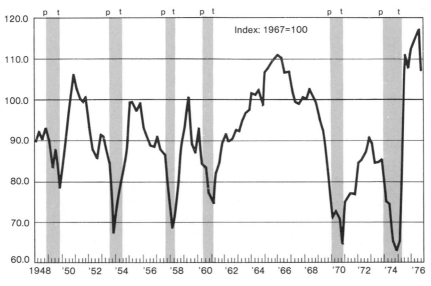

Figure 5-2. Profit-type income per unit of output, nonfinancial corporate business (1967=100)

Sources: U.S. Department of Labor; U.S. Department of Commerce; Conference Board.

search. (See Fig. 5-1 relating to the U.S. nonfinancial corporate business sector.) The figure shows that the ratio has invariably led at the upper turning points since 1948—by many quarters in the longer expansions, although there were usually secondary peaks in the ratio a few quarters before the turns in business activity. The ratio has usually, but not invariably, turned up before the reference cycle troughs. Although the ratio was coincident at the troughs in 1949 and 1961, there were secondary troughs 2 and 3 quarters prior to the reference cycle troughs, respectively, even in these contractions.

Although labor is only part of total factor cost (exclusive of profit), albeit the major part, profits per unit of output (Fig. 5-2) show much the same cyclical pattern as the ratio of price to unit labor costs as far as timing is concerned, but not amplitude. The one exception was in the 1969-70 contraction, when unit profits were coincident at the trough, although there was a secondary trough 3 quarters earlier, at the time the ratio made its primary trough.

The estimates developed in this study make possible a useful extension of the analysis developed by Mitchell and his followers. In addition to unit labor costs, we are able to analyze the cyclical behavior of fixed capital costs per unit of output and then total unit cost in relation to price in terms of the corresponding factor price and productivity components. In the following sections, we shall first analyze the cyclical movements of unit labor costs in terms of the price of labor and labor productivity components, and the unit fixed capital costs in the same way. Then, based on a combination of both the labor and capital components, we are able to describe the behavior of unit total factor cost viewed as the quotient of total factor price and TFP, and then the ratio of unit total factor cost to price. This ratio comes much closer than the unit labor cost/price ratio to describing the movements of unit profits—the variable of particular significance for understanding cycles.[3]

It must be remembered, however, that gross factor costs are not quite the same as gross product originating in a sector or industry. The difference is indirect business taxes (less subsidies). Accordingly, we also look at unit net indirect business taxes and unit total cost. But since the taxes are only about 10 percent of sector gross product in recent years, and less earlier, we find that the patterns of changes in total unit cost and in unit factor cost are almost the same.

The analysis that follows is largely in terms of timing—quarters of lead or lag, or coincidence, of the several variables compared with the reference cycle turning points. Relative rates of change of the related variables are also involved, of course. (These are computed over a 2 quarter span). To simplify the description of timing relationships, the series have been averaged for all cycles from 1948 through 1976, and are summarized in Table 5-5. The numbers relate to the quarters of lead (-) or lag between the primary turning points of a series and the reference cycle turns. The numbers in parentheses relate to leads or lags of the secondary turning points of the specific series, but these are confined to peak periods, since contractions are generally too short to contain more than one trough in a given series. Our description is in terms of average timing of the several variables (Figs. 5-3 and 5-4). Leads and lags over successive cycles since 1948 have varied somewhat, but show much of the same net effect on unit profits in each, as noted earlier.

Output and Unit Labor Costs

In considering the cyclical relationship between unit costs and prices (Table 5-5a) it must be noted that the rate of increase in output itself peaks 5 quarters before the upper turning point of the cycle, on average, with a secondary (lower) peak leading by 2 quarters. The peak in rates of change in output per hour occurs at least 6 quarters prior to the upper turning point, with a secondary peak that leads by 3 quarters. Thus, productivity advance decelerates *before* output begins to slow. Rates of change in average hourly labor com-

---

[3]The relationship is even closer to profits as a percent of gross product.

Table 5-5. U.S. nonfinancial corporate sector: cyclical timing of
average rates of change in productivity, factor price, unit cost, and
product price variables relative to reference cycle turning points, 1948-76

	No. of quarters lead (-) lag		
	Peak		Trough
Part a. Labor variables, output, and prices.			
Real product (output)	−5	(−2)	0
Output per labor hour	−6	(−3)	−1
Average hourly labor compensation	−5	(−2)	0
Unit labor cost	2	(−1)	−1
Implicit price deflator	−2	(−6)	−2
Ratio of price to unit labor cost	−6	(−3)	−1
Part b. Cyclical timing of rates of change in capital variables.			
Output per unit of capital	−5	(−2)	0
Price of capital	−2	(2)	0
Unit capital costs	3	(2)	0
Ratio of price to unit capital cost	−5	(−1)	0
Part c. Cyclical timing of rates of change in total factor variables and ratios of price to unit costs.			
Total factor productivity	−6	(−2)	−1
Average factor price	−2	(−5)	0
Unit factor cost	2	(1)	−1
Unit indirect business taxes	3	(1)	−1
Unit total cost (factors and taxes)	3	(1)	−1
Ratio of price to unit factor cost	−6	(−3)	−1
Ratio of price to unit total cost	−6	(−3)	−1
Unit profits	−5	−	−1

Note: Numbers in parentheses refer to secondary peaks in rates of change, which are lower than the primary peaks.

pensation peak with a 5-quarter lead and a secondary peak 3 quarters after that coinciding with the peaks in rates of output change. But the rates of change in labor productivity generally decelerate faster than average hourly earnings until 2 quarters after the peak, so unit labor cost changes lag at the upper turning point, although there is a minor down-tick 1 quarter in advance. Although increases in the product price deflator peak 2 quarters prior to the reference peak, on average, unit labor cost increases are greater than price increases for at least a year before that, so changes in the ratio of price to unit labor cost begin declining at least 6 quarters in advance of the cycle turning point.

At the trough, average rates of change in output bottom out coincidentally with the reference cycle. So, too, do changes in average hourly labor compensation. But changes in real product per hour rise 1 quarter prior to the cycle trough, on average, and enough so as to push changes in unit labor cost down and increase the ratio of price to unit labor cost prior to the trough. This contributes to the widening of profit margins, helping to set the stage for recovery.

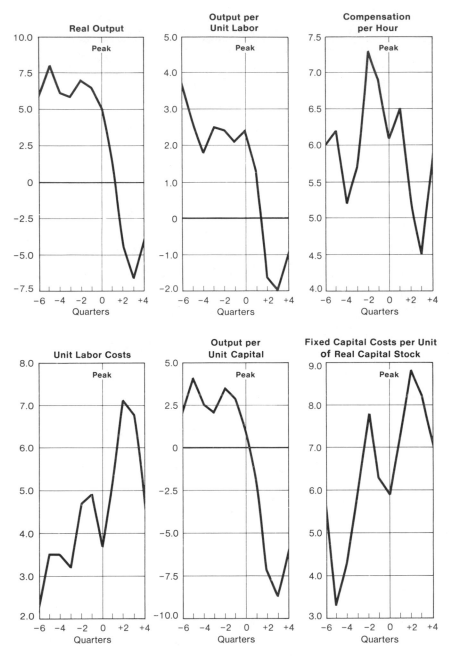

Figure 5-3. U.S. nonfinancial corporate sector average quarterly rates of change in productivity and related variables* 6 quarters before and 4 quarters after cycle peaks, 1948-76

*Average annual percentage rates of change over 2-quarter spans.

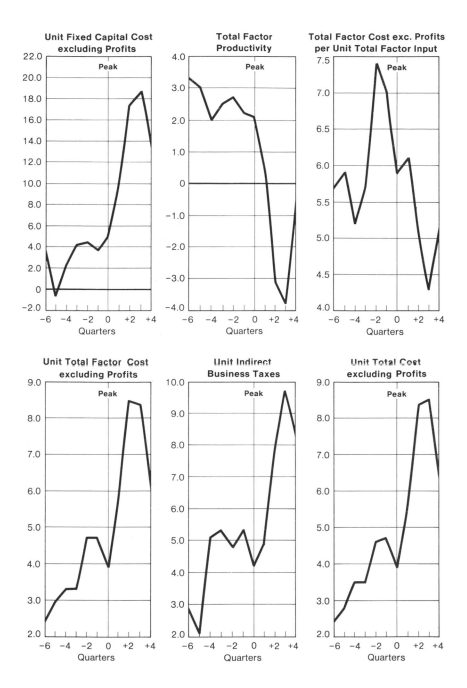

Sources: U.S. Department of Labor; U.S. Department of Commerce; Conference Board.

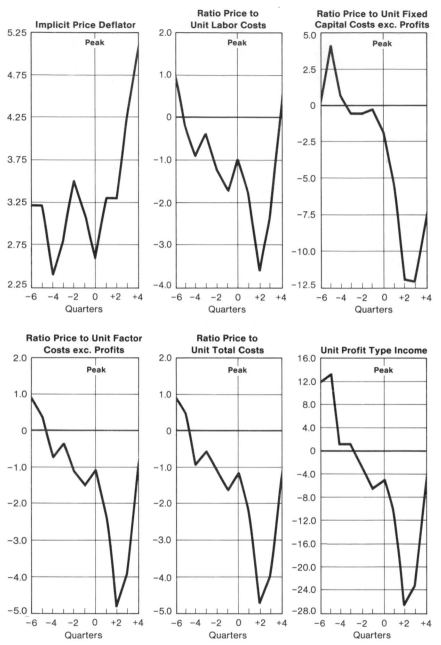

Fig. 5-3 (cont.)

Unit Capital Costs

Our new estimates of capital stocks, inputs, productivity, and the average price of capital make possible the analysis of the cyclical role of this element (Table 5-5b). As might be expected, rates of change in output per unit of capital have much the same pattern as changes in output itself, since stocks of capital cannot be adjusted rapidly to changes in rates of production. Thus, changes in the output-capital ratio peak 5 quarters before the reference cycle peak—the same lead as output changes. Changes in the price of capital—which it will be recalled reflected both interest rates and the replacement prices of the underlying capital goods—peak 2 quarters in advance of the reference turn. But changes in the output-capital ratio decelerate faster than those in the price of capital, so that the peak change in unit capital costs lags the cycle peak by three quarters. Unit capital costs are rising faster than prices generally for 5 quarters prior to the cycle peak. Thus, for more than a year before the upper turning point, unit capital costs join labor costs in pressing against prices and squeezing profit margins.

Changes in the ratio of price to unit capital costs do not help bring about the recovery, however, since they are a coincident indicator at the trough. Although the rate of increase in product prices picks up 2 quarters prior to the trough, it still does not pull ahead of the rate of increase of unit capital costs until the trough has been reached—in contrast to the 1-quarter lead of the ratio of price to unit labor costs. But the increase in the ratio of price to unit capital costs helps reinforce the recovery once begun.

Unit Total Costs, Prices, and Profits

The new capital and TFP estimates (Table 5-5c) also make it possible to analyze the behavior of combined labor and capital costs per unit of output as the quotient of total factor price and total factor productivity. The ratio of price to unit factor costs plus unit indirect business taxes provides a good approximation to unit profits of the sector, as we shall see shortly.

As shown in Table 5-5c, rates of change in the ratios of price to unit factor costs and to unit total costs show the same leads at reference cycle peaks and troughs as the ratio of price to unit labor costs—at least 6 quarters at the peak and 1 quarter at the trough. This is not surprising in view of the preponderant weight of labor in total costs. But the timing of the component variables differs slightly in a few instances from the timing of the labor variables. Rates of change in TFP show the same leads as those in output per

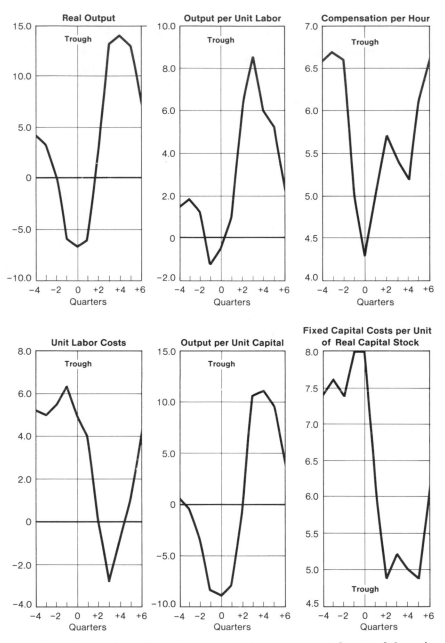

Figure 5-4. U. S. nonfinancial corporate sector average quarterly rates of change in productivity and related variables 4 quarters before and 6 quarters after cycle troughs, 1948-76

Sources: U.S. Department of Labor; U.S. Department of Commerce; Conference Board.

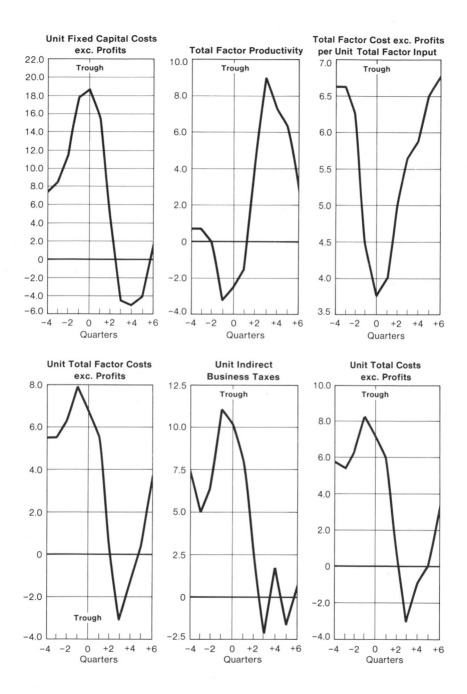

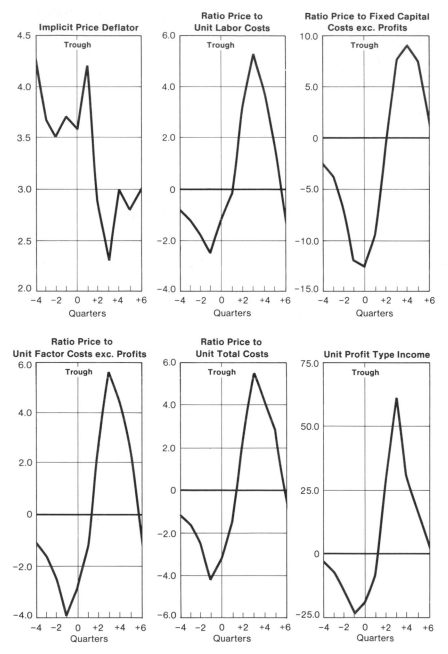

Fig. 5-4 (cont.)

hour, except that the secondary peak of the former shows a 2-quarter lead instead of a 3-quarter lead. This reflects the fact that changes in the output/capital ratio show 1-quarter less lead than changes in the output/labor ratio. Also, changes in average factor price show a 2-quarter lead over the reference cycle peak, the same as changes in the price of capital, rather than the 5-quarter lead of changes in average hourly compensation. But the latter is reflected in a secondary peak of changes in average factor prices 5 quarters before the reference cycle turning point. Changes in all factor prices are coincident at the trough.

Changes in unit factor costs show a 2-quarter average lag over the reference cycle peak, which became an average 1-quarter lead at the trough, the same as for the labor variables. It is the drop in unit cost changes, reflecting the acceleration in productivity prior to the trough that increases the ratio of price to unit costs and widens profit margins. Changes in productivity continue to accelerate, and changes in unit factor costs continue to decelerate for several quarters after the trough, contributing to the rapid recovery of profits during the early phase of expansion.

Changes in unit total costs have a 3-quarter average lag after the peak, compared with 2 for unit factor cost, reflecting the 3-quarter lag of changes in indirect business taxes (less subsidies) per unit of output. But this still represents an average 1-quarter lead over the trough. And changes in the ratio of price to unit total costs show the same average leads at the peak and trough as those in the ratio of price to unit factor costs.

As would be expected, the timing of changes in the price to unit total cost ratio is virtually the same as that in changes in unit profits. They both show the 1-quarter lead at the trough, although unit profits have a 5-quarter lead at the peak compared with 6-quarter lead in changes of the ratio. It is the unit-profit lead at both turning points, of course, that is the crucial element in helping to turn business activity around by affecting the stock market and investment commitments that are also leading indicators.[4]

The timing of turning points in productivity, factor prices, unit costs, the price/cost ratios, and unit profits has varied somewhat over the six cycles since 1948. But in virtually all of the particular cycles, the interrelated behavior of these variables has contributed to the reversal of periods of both expansion and contraction as has been explained with reference to their average cyclical behavior. Certainly, an understanding of the causal forces behind the cyclical behavior of the productivity-cost-price nexus is essential to the development of policies to promote steadier economic growth.

[4] U.S. Department of Commerce, *Business Conditions Digest* (Washington, D.C.: Government Printing Office), a monthly publication of cyclical economic indicators.

CHAPTER 6

Causal Analysis of Productivity Change within Manufacturing Industries

Gains in output beyond increases in tangible inputs are due to many causes, such as technological advances, increases in knowledge, innovative activity, and other factors mentioned in Chapter 2. Many of these influences on changes in productivity are quantitative and, therefore, measurable, at least in principle, while others are not. For example, research and development expenditures can be quantified, but changes in work-related values cannot be. In this chapter an effort is made to examine statistically the impact of quantifiable—and available—factors influencing productivity change.

Rates of growth in total factor productivity (TFP) vary substantially across industries (Chapter 3, Table 3-5). By analyzing this variation one is able to get a handle on the influence of quantitative factors with respect to differences in their levels or rates of change, which may explain why productivity growth rates differ among industries. Specifically, an attempt is made to explain the variation in 1948-76 rates of change of TFP among the twenty two-digit SIC (Standard Industrial Code) manufacturing industries through the use of multiple regression methods.

Such a causal analysis of TFP was first reported by Kendrick[1] where he examined cross-sectionally the relationship between rates of growth of TFP and nine explanatory variables: rate of change in output; rate of change in real capital; variability of output changes; average education per employee;

[1] John W. Kendrick, *Postwar Productivity Trends in the United States, 1948-1969* (New York: National Bureau of Economic Research, 1973).

ratio of research and development (R&D) expenditures to sales; average hours worked; degree of concentration of each industry; rate of change in concentration; and degree of unionization. The first two variables, rates of change in output and real capital, are included to account for scalar effects, as is the cyclical variability of output. The remaining variables allow for the influences of the stock of human capital, technological advances, and the market power of firms and unions.

Kendrick's results indicate that productivity rates of change across manufacturing industries can best be explained by the rate of change in output and, negatively, by the degree of unionization. Kendrick points out that using the rate of change of output is circular for output is a result as well as a cause of productivity. As productivity rises relatively, unit costs and relative prices decline, thereby encouraging sales or higher output (Chapter 4). The rate of change in output is, therefore, only partially successful at capturing scalar effects. Further, output is highly correlated with the R&D ratio and the education variable. Therefore, output was dropped from the regression. The final result of Kendrick's regression analysis was a positive relationship between productivity and average education and a negative relationship with the degree of unionization.

A more recent study by Terleckyj[2] uses Kendrick's estimates of productivity rates of change. In this work, Terleckyj modifies the R&D variable in several respects. First, R&D funds are, where possible, attributed to the industry on a product basis, which parallels the establishment allocation of output in the productivity estimates. Second, R&D funds are separated into government funded dollars and privately funded dollars, which are then taken as a ratio to value-added, rather than sales. Terleckyj also derived a second set of R&D data, R&D embodied in intermediate goods and R&D embodied in capital goods.

Terleckyj introduces an additional variable to those already examined by Kendrick, the proportion of sales to nongovernment customers (i.e., private sales). He then regresses productivity on private sales, degree of unionization, a measure of cyclical instability, and his various measures of R&D expenditures. For manufacturing, Terleckyj concludes that the most promising equation includes the degree of unionization, privately funded R&D ratio, and R&D embodied in producers' goods. The private sales, cyclical instability, and government financed R&D ratio variables are also included, but are not significant.

[2]Nestor E. Terleckyj, *Effects of R&D on the Productivity Growth of Industries: An Exploratory Study* (Washington, D.C.: National Planning Association, 1974).

In this study these and other variables are included:[3]

1. Average rate of capacity utilization: The 1948-76 average of the Wharton capacity utilization index is used to capture the variability of intensity of capital use. An alternative version adjusts the average for the preferred operating rate reported by the Bureau of Census for 1973.
2. Average absolute derivation from the mean capacity utilization index: A measure of cyclical variation in the use of capital.
3. Median education in 1958 and 1972: A proxy measure of the stock of human capital.
4. Privately funded applied R&D as a percent of gross product originating: Privately funded R&D ratios are available for 1958, 1967, 1972, and 1974; the 1958 to 1972 change in the R&D ratio is also included, as is R&D embodied in intermediate goods.
5. Average hours worked: The 1948-76 average of hours worked per week is included to indicate possible differences in the quality of effort.
6. Concentration ratios for 1947, 1967, and 1972: The weighted (by value of total shipments) average percent of sales of the top four companies within each four digit SIC industry is used to account for changes in economic (allocative) efficiency.
7. Unionization ratio: Kendrick's estimate for 1958 of percentage of employees that are union members is updated for 1968 and 1972. Also included is the rate of change in the unionization ratio.
8. Percent of man-days idled due to work stoppages: The 1948-76 average and average deviation are calculated from Department of Labor annual series to account for the effect of days lost and disruptions due to work stoppages.
9. Pollution abatement expenditures as a percent of capital expenditures: Based on the establishment census conducted in 1973, this variable is a proxy for the impact of legislated and purportedly nonproductive additions to capital stock.
10. Composition of work force by sex: The female proportion of all employees is included to capture the effect of this less experienced and, presumedly, less productive group as indicated by relative pay and value-added per annum. Also included in the analysis is the rate of change in the proportion of women.
11. Composition of work force by production versus salaried workers: The ratio of production workers to all employees is included to determine

---

[3]The derivation and specific sources of each variable are available upon request from The Conference Board, 845 Third Avenue, New York, New York, 10022.

whether the trend toward fewer production workers, in relative terms, has an impact on productivity change.

12. Composition of work force by age: The median age in 1972 is included to capture the effect of experience. Changes in this variable over time should be examined, but it is not available for earlier periods.

13. Layoff rate: The 1958-76 average layoffs per 100 employees and the average absolute deviation are included to capture the degree of uncertainty of future employment or cyclicality facing workers.

14. Quit rate: The 1958-76 average quits per 100 employees and the average absolute deviation are included to account for the confidence workers may have in their ability to change jobs and a measure of mobility. The quit rate may also be a negatively related proxy for the degree of absenteeism.

15. Shift of employment among industries: The rate of change from 1958 to 1976 of the proportion of employment in each industry, as a percent of total manufacturing, is used to account for intrasectoral shifts.

Since the rate of change in output was not included in this study because of its circular relationship with productivity, an alternative measure of scalar effects, the level of output in the base year (1972) was included. An additional variable used to capture scalar effects is the 1948-76 rate of growth in total factor input.

The simple correlation coefficients between the 1948-76 rates of change[4] in TFP and the above variables across the twenty manufacturing industries are, for the most part, insignificant. Table 6-1 presents the simple correlation co-efficients of those variables that are significantly correlated with 1948-76 growth rates of TFP across manufacturing industries.[5] As expected, the rate of change in real output (1948-76) is highly correlated with TFP. The two variables that are included to capture the impact of unions on TFP, percent man-days idled due to work stoppages (MDI) and percent of employment member of unions (UN58), are both negatively related to TFP at the 5 percent level. Also, research and development spending, both privately funded (RDEM58) and embodied in intermediate goods (RDG58), as well as their sum (R&D58), are positively correlated with TFP.

[4] Because of the severe 1973-75 recession, the choice of 1976 as the end point in calculating the long-term productivity rates of change may unduly influence the results of this analysis. However, the regression results for the 1949-73 and 1953-73 periods show no substantial differences.

[5] For twenty observations, the correlation coefficient is statistically significant at the 5 percent level for correlation equal to or greater than 0.423, and 0.360 at the 1 percent level.

Table 6-1. Simple correlation coefficients of significant variables on rates of growth of total factor productivity, 20 manufacturing industries

Variable	Correlation with TFP4876
OUT4876	0.601[a]
MDI	−0.556[a]
UN58	−0.471[a]
R&D58	0.388[b]
RDEM58	0.370[b]
RDG58	0.363[b]
TFP4866	0.915[a]
TFP6676	0.792[b]

Between TFP4866 and TFP6676 0.478

Where:

OUT4876 = Rate of change in output, 1948-76
MDI   = Percent of man-days idled due to work stoppages, 1948-74 average
UN58   = Percent of employment union members, 1958
R&D58   = Private-funded R&D (RDG58) plus R&D embodied in intermediate goods (RDEM58) as a percent of gross product originating, 1958
TFP   = Rate of change in total factor productivity:
            4876 − 1948 to 1976
            4866 − 1948 to 1966
            6676 − 1966 to 1976

[a]Significant at the 5% level.
[b]Significant at the 10% level.

These three significant variables, MDI, UN58 and R&D58, are included in a regression analysis of TFP, and the results (Table 6-2) indicate that man-days idled is significantly and negatively related to TFP, and R&D58 positively so. However, the unionization ratio is insignificant, but this result is due to the high correlation between UN58 and MDI. Dropping UN58 does not significantly affect the overall results: about half of the variation in TFP growth rates over the postwar period can be explained by variations in the 1948-76 average of man-days idled due to work stoppages, and R&D spending as a percent of gross product originating in 1958.

A variable may be a significant factor in regression analysis even though its simple correlation is weak, because other factors that are accounted for in regression analysis may cloud the relationship when measured by simple correlation. Therefore, all of the possible variables mentioned above are included in the multiple regression analysis. However, because of severe intercorrelation among many of the explanatory variables, some of the candidates are significant in some cases and not in others. Therefore, there are several regressions to choose from. The "best" equation in terms of explaining variations in productivity change among manufacturing industries, is shown in Table 6-3.

Table 6-2. Multiple regression results: cross-sectional analysis,* using significant variables on rates of growth of total factor productivity, 20 manufacturing industries

A-1. Variables with significant correlation coefficients

Variable	Coefficient	t-statistic
Constant	2.97540	4.850
MDI	−1.28014	−2.657
R&D58	0.13826	2.954
UN58	−0.01364	−0.979
R^2=0.576	$\bar{R}^2$=0.497	SEE=0.625

A-2. Excluding unionization ratio

Variable	Coefficient	t-statistic
Constant	2.43026	9.442
MDI	−1.54647	−3.894
R&D58	−0.14121	3.027
R^2=0.551	$\bar{R}^2$=0.498	SEE=0.624

Where:

MDI = Man-days idled due to work stoppages, percent of the hours, 1948-74 average

R&D58 = Private-funded applied R&D plus R&D embodied in intermediate goods as a percent of gross product originating, 1958

UN58 = Percent of employment union members, 1958

R^2 = Coefficient of determination

$\bar{R}^2$ = Coefficient of determination, corrected for degrees of freedom

SEE – Standard error of the estimate

*Dependent variable is 1948-76 compound rate of growth in TFP.

About 86 percent of the variation in productivity trends within manufacturing is explained by the degree of unionization, its rate of growth, R&D spending, degree of concentration, cyclical variation in the utilization of capital, and women as a percent of all employees. Even though percent man-days idled is significant in the simpler equation (Table 6-2), in the presence of these additional explanatory factors, it becomes insignificant and the unionization ratio becomes significant. This type of sensitivity of some variables to the presence of other variables demonstrates the difficulty in statistically establishing the causes of variation in productivity growth when severe multicollinearity exists.

The negative relationship between productivity and the percentage of employees belonging to unions is not surprising in view of the restrictive work rules of many unions and other aspects of labor-management relationships that may hinder greater efficiency. Unionization may, in part, be accounting for the influence of other variables as well. It is significantly related to the lay-off rate, indicating that there is a tendency for higher rates of lay-offs in more highly unionized industries and that these industries are associated with

*Table 6-3. Regression results: cross-sectional analysis of
productivity growth in 20 manufacturing industries, 1948-76 ("best" equation)*

A.   Regression results

Dependent variable: 1948-76 growth of total factor productivity[a]

Variable	Coefficient	t-statistic
Constant	3.19069	6.797
UN58	−0.03572	−4.210
%UN5872	0.17591	4.492
R&D58	0.18295	4.966
CR58	0.01905	2.719
WABS4876	−0.18553	−3.674
PW66	0.01579	2.960
R^2=0.859	$\bar{R}^2$=0.793	SER=0.400

B.   Simple correlation coefficients

	TFP4876	UN58	%UN5872	R&D58	CR58	WABS4876	PW66
TFP4876	1.000						
UN58	−0.471[b]	1.000					
%UN5872	0.226	−0.035	1.000				
R&D58	0.388[c]	0.46	−0.332	1.000			
CR58	0.097	0.425[b]	−0.366[c]	0.461[b]	1.000		
WABS4876	−0.251	0.197	−0.037	0.375[c]	0.312	1.000	
PW66	0.329	−0.159	0.074	−0.236	−0.120	−0.196	1.000

Where:

%UN5872= 1958-72 rate of change in percent of employment members of unions
CR58   = Concentration ratio based on weighted value of shipments, 1958
WABS4876=Average absolute deviation of Wharton capacity utilization index, 1948-76
PW66   = Women as a percent of all employees, 1966
Other variables as noted in Table 6-2.

[a]Compound annual average rate of change.
[b]Significant at the 5 percent level.
[c]Significant at the 10 percent level.

lower rates of productivity advances. There is also a negative correlation between unionization and the 1948-76 rate of change in total factor inputs, indicating that the more highly unionized industries have invested at slower relative rates, possibly because they are the more mature industries.

A striking result is the strong, positive relationship between the 1958-72 rate of change in unionization and the rate of productivity advances. However, it is difficult to explain the positive effect this variable (%UN5872) has on productivity. Probably it is picking up the positive effects of other factors, such as higher concentration ratios in industries that are experiencing faster gains in unionization. There is a strong correlation between %UN5872 and a number of other variables: quit rate, lay-off rate, median age, percent production workers, percent women employees, privately funded R&D spending, concentration ratio, median education, and rate of growth in total factor input. Because of these intercorrelations it is difficult to separate out the effect of this variable.

The percent change in unionization is also correlated with its level (UN58), yet in its absence the level of unionization remains significantly related to productivity, but the concentration ratio (CR58) becomes insignificant. Dropping %UN5872 from the regression does lower the explanatory power of the equation to 64 percent, indicating that the rate of change in unionization is a powerful variable in explaining advances in productivity.

The strong, positive relationship between the privately funded applied R&D ratio and productivity changes is consistent with both Kendrick's and Terleckyj's results, as is the role of R&D embodied in intermediate goods.

The concentration ratio (CR58) also has a positive relationship to rates of productivity advances. This variable may be, in part, accounting for scalar effects for it is significantly correlated to level of output in 1972 as well as R&D. It is also positively related to the quit rate, median age and average education that are indicators of higher levels of mobility, experience, and education.

Variability in the use of capital facilities, as measured by the average absolute deviation of the Wharton capacity utilization rate (WABS4876), has the expected negative relationship with rates of change in TFP across manufacturing industries. Apparently, the more cyclically stable industries are better able to achieve productivity gains, whereas highly cyclical industries must keep on hand less productive or marginal facilities for use during peak periods. Other related factors are loss of economies of scale during slack periods and, in contrast, loss of efficiency due to bottlenecks when facilities are used to their limit. Interestingly, the average level of capacity utilization is not a significant variable, since this factor is more closely dependent upon the type of production process (continuous versus batch) than efficiency in the use of the facilities.

The last variable that proved significant is the percent of all employees that are women (PW66). The positive relationship of this variable is surprising, since this group is less experienced and, therefore, would be expected to have a negative impact on productivity gain. However, variability in the proportion of women across industries does not measure this negative impact on productivity. Such a negative influence is exhibited, however, by the rate of change in the proportion of women (%PW), a measure of those industries that are gaining a relatively greater proportion of women: %PW has a negative correlation with TFP. (In one variation of the equation, %PW was substituted for the level of the proportion of women. It proved to be a significant negative factor on TFP.)

The level of women as a percent of all employees does not, therefore, capture the increase in less experienced employees, but is capturing other effects on TFP. In 1950, women were 25.7 percent of all manufacturing employees. This proportion had increased to 29.5 percent by 1976. Yet, correlations between the proportion of women in 1950, 1966, and 1976 are all positive with respect to growth rates of productivity. It appears that the proportion of women is showing some positive influences on productivity gains. For instance, industries with higher proportions of women may be the more "enlightened" type of industries that are more prone to take advantage of technological and managerial advances. The proportion of women may also be a reflection of the type of production process of the industry. For example, women in the apparel industry have traditionally comprised over three-fourths of its labor force. The leather, textile, and electrical equipment industries have traditionally employed large proportions of women. These industries are the type that require considerable "hand" work in their assembly-type production. Therefore, the effect of small substitutions of capital for labor in these industries would likely result in relatively larger gains in productivity.

Even though about 86 percent of the variation in TFP has been explained by the factors described above, other factors are also important in determining productivity advances, but are not highlighted using multiple regression methods either because of severe intercorrelations or lack of data, such as percent of man-days idle due to work stoppage.

Another important contributor to productivity is education, as shown earlier by Kendrick and Denison.[6] Unfortunately, there is not sufficient history of attained educational levels by industry to determine whether industry rates of growth in productivity are related to rates of growth in average education. Apparently, the level of education in a given year bears little relationship with productivity change across industries. This is not to say that the level of education is unimportant, but that the level is not the correct measure of educational attainment in this type of analysis.

Other measures of labor quality, in addition to education, are the quit and layoff rates. These measure the mobility of the work force and the certainty of continued employment, or, stated differently, the cyclicality of employment. Both variables are related to productivity, the quit rate in a negative fashion, and the layoff rate positively. The negative impact of the quit rate is another indication that the more cyclical or volatile industries tend to have slower growth in productivity, a relationship also indicated by

[6]Edward Denison, *Accounting for U.S. Economic Growth 1929-1969* (Washington, D.C.: The Brookings Institution, 1974).

the capacity utilization (WABS) variable. The positive influence of layoffs is also as expected. Industries with higher than average layoff rates apparently are able to reduce their work forces during periods of business slowdowns, thereby minimizing the negative impact on productivity of a decline in output and its labor utilization. These industries, because of the characteristics of their operations, are probably less affected by negative displacement effects when they choose to lay off workers during slower periods such that, when they choose to retire, there is relatively little loss of efficiency. Other industries may find it to their advantage in the long run to keep their work force intact and suffer a short-term efficiency loss during economic slowdowns.

Of course, there are a number of factors that influence productivity advances that have not been examined due to the lack of data, such as workers' years of experience, on-the-job training, health care, and the changing quality of capital. This last factor is usually measured by the age of capital. Since capital is continually being replaced with more productive plant and equipment, as the average age of capital declines it is expected that productivity would rise. Unfortunately, data on the age of capital by industry are not available.

One other area to be considered is the influence of government mandated pollution abatement expenditures and costs incurred in meeting Occupational Safety and Health Act regulations. Since the experience of adjusting to these demands on investment funds (which are added to capital input) has been short (reliable data on pollution abatement expenditures by industry is only available since 1973), no conclusion can be drawn as to their long-term impact on productivity, though there is evidence[7] that there have been short-term negative impacts.

Examining the 1966-76 Slowdown

In this section, some of the factors that may have contributed to the slowdown in TFP since 1966 are examined, again using multiple regression methods applied to the manufacturing industries.

The factors used in the regression discussed above could be looked upon as the factors that affect long-run trends in productivity growth. Therefore,

[7]John G. Myers, "The new realities in productivity and growth: Energy and pollution," *Business Economics* (January 1977): 53-57; John G. Myers, *et al.*, "The Impact of OPEC, FEA, EPA and OSHA on Productivity and Growth," The Conference Board *Record* (April 1976).

*Table 6-4. Regression results: cross-sectional analysis of
productivity growth in 20 manufacturing industries, 1948-66 and 1966-76*

Dependent variable: 1948-66 total factor productivity*

Variable	Coefficient	t-statistic
Constant	3.92888	5.471
UN58	−0.04730	−3.830
%UN5868	0.10410	2.615
R&D58	0.14139	2.668
CR58	0.02176	2.092
WABS4866	−0.08433	−1.134
PW50	0.00610	0.732
R^2=0.747	$\bar{R}^2$=0.631	SEE=0.582

Dependent variable: 1966-76 total factor productivity*

Variable	Coefficient	t-statistic
Constant	−1.38540	−1.319
UN72	0.03515	−2.157
%UN6872	−0.03241	−0.611
R&D74	0.10875	1.813
CR72	0.00806	0.532
WABS6676	−0.20091	−1.973
PW76	0.04000	3.483
R^2=0.600	$\bar{R}^2$=0.416	SEE=0.857

*For definitions of variables see Tables 6-2 and 6-3; specific dates of variables are as noted.

if these factors are also able to successfully explain the short 1966-76 period, when productivity slowed drastically in many industries (Table 3-5), then this result would indicate that the nature of the slowdown may be considered as fairly permanent. That is, we have entered a period of slower long-run productivity growth because of changes in productivity's underlying causes, and are not just experiencing a subperiod of slower gains due to erratic or unmeasured forces.

The above regression was run for two subperiods, 1948-66 and 1966-76. Where possible, the explanatory variables were adjusted to coincide with these two subperiods. The results are presented in Table 6-4. For the 1948-66 subperiod the results are very similar to the regression over the entire period, except that the measure of cyclical variability (WABS) and the proportion of women are not significantly related to TFP. Also, about 75 percent of the variation is explained, about eleven percentage points less than the full period regression.

For the equation covering the post-1966 period, about 60 percent of the variation in productivity is explained. During this period of slower productivity growth, the measure of cyclicality (WABS) and the proportion of women (PW) are now statistically significant. However, the rate of change in unionization (%UN), and concentration (CR) are now insignificant. R&D spending is significant, but to a lesser degree. Surprisingly, the unionization ratio is now positively and significantly related to advances in TFP, though this result may be due to problems of measuring unionization.

The implication of these two equations is that there is no conclusive evidence that the slowdown will be of a long-lasting nature, since the underlying factors of productivity gains—as identified here—are unstable. Only R&D spending is consistent in all three equations covering the full-period and two subperiods. The unionization ratio changes its relationship in the post-1966 period, and the other variables are insignificant in either the earlier or later subperiods.

Appendix Tables

LIST OF SECTORS AND INDUSTRIES

Private Domestic Business Economy
Total Manufacturing
Nonfarm Nonmanufacturing
Farming
Mining
Contract Construction
Total Transportation
  Railroad Transportation
  Nonrail Transportation
Communications
Public Utilities
Trade
Finance and Insurance
Real Estate
Services
Food
Tobacco
Textiles

Apparel
Lumber
Furniture
Paper
Printing and Publishing
Chemicals
Petroleum
Rubber
Leather
Stone, Clay and Glass
Primary Metals
Fabricated Metals
Machinery except Electrical
Electrical Machinery
Transportation Equipment
Instruments
Miscellaneous Manufactures

PRIVATE DOMESTIC BUSINESS ECONOMY

OUTPUT, INPUTS, AND PRODUCTIVITY RATIOS
(1967=100)

	REAL OUTPUT	LABOR INPUT	CAPITAL INPUT	TOTAL FACTOR INPUT	TOTAL FACTOR PRODUCTIVITY
1948	48.8	93.5	63.2	82.7	59.1
1949	48.2	90.3	64.4	81.0	59.5
1950	52.8	91.2	66.7	82.5	64.0
1951	56.0	93.9	69.1	85.0	65.8
1952	57.8	93.9	70.7	85.6	67.5
1953	60.4	94.7	72.0	86.6	69.7
1954	59.6	91.5	73.2	85.0	70.2
1955	64.5	94.8	75.5	87.9	73.4
1956	66.5	96.2	77.7	89.6	74.3
1957	67.6	94.6	79.7	89.3	75.6
1958	66.4	90.2	81.1	87.0	76.4
1959	71.3	93.4	82.7	89.6	79.5
1960	72.7	93.6	84.1	90.2	80.6
1961	74.0	91.1	85.5	89.1	83.0
1962	78.6	93.4	87.3	91.2	86.2
1963	82.1	93.8	89.1	92.1	89.2
1964	86.7	95.1	91.3	93.8	92.5
1965	92.8	98.1	93.9	96.6	96.0
1966	97.9	100.3	97.2	99.2	98.7
1967	100.0	100.0	100.0	100.0	100.0
1968	105.2	101.8	103.0	102.2	102.9
1969	108.5	104.5	106.5	105.2	103.1
1970	107.9	102.8	109.2	105.0	102.8
1971	110.9	102.3	111.9	105.5	105.1
1972	118.2	106.0	114.8	109.0	108.5
1973	125.0	110.1	118.5	112.9	110.7
1974	122.7	110.6	121.3	114.2	107.5
1975	120.6	106.1	122.3	111.5	108.2
1976	128.9	108.9	124.4	114.1	113.0
1977	135.8	113.7	128.4	118.3	114.9
1978P	141.5	118.2	132.2	122.9	115.1

PRIVATE DOMESTIC BUSINESS ECONOMY *(continued)*

OUTPUT, INPUTS, AND PRODUCTIVITY RATIOS
(1967=100)

	REAL OUTPUT	LABOR INPUT	CAPITAL INPUT	TOTAL FACTOR INPUT	TOTAL FACTOR PRODUCTIVITY
1948 I	48.0	93.4	61.0	82.2	58.4
1948 II	49.0	92.9	61.7	82.1	59.6
1948 III	48.8	93.7	62.4	82.9	58.9
1948 IV	49.5	93.2	63.2	82.9	59.8
1949 I	48.5	92.0	62.8	81.9	59.2
1949 II	48.1	91.2	63.4	81.6	58.9
1949 III	48.4	89.5	63.9	80.7	60.0
1949 IV	47.8	88.0	64.4	79.9	59.9
1950 I	50.0	88.3	64.6	80.2	62.4
1950 II	52.0	90.4	65.3	81.8	63.6
1950 III	54.1	92.5	66.0	83.4	64.9
1950 IV	55.0	93.2	66.7	84.1	65.4
1951 I	55.1	94.1	67.2	84.8	64.9
1951 II	55.6	94.3	67.8	85.2	65.3
1951 III	56.5	93.1	68.5	84.7	66.7
1951 IV	56.8	93.5	69.1	85.1	66.8
1952 I	57.1	94.0	69.2	85.5	66.0
1952 II	57.3	92.7	69.8	84.9	67.5
1952 III	57.6	92.9	70.2	85.2	67.7
1952 IV	59.3	95.3	70.7	86.9	68.2
1953 I	60.4	95.8	70.6	87.2	69.2
1953 II	60.9	95.4	71.1	87.1	70.0
1953 III	60.6	94.4	71.5	86.6	70.0
1953 IV	59.7	92.8	72.0	85.7	69.7
1954 I	59.0	92.3	72.2	85.5	69.0
1954 II	58.8	91.0	72.4	84.7	69.4
1954 III	59.7	90.6	72.8	84.6	70.6
1954 IV	61.1	91.3	73.2	85.2	71.7
1955 I	62.8	92.8	73.9	86.4	72.6
1955 II	64.2	93.8	74.4	87.2	73.6
1955 III	65.1	95.4	74.9	88.4	73.6
1955 IV	66.0	96.6	75.5	89.4	73.8
1956 I	66.0	96.0	75.9	89.2	74.0
1956 II	66.5	96.3	76.5	89.6	74.1
1956 III	66.3	96.0	77.1	89.6	74.0
1956 IV	67.3	95.6	77.7	89.6	75.1
1957 I	67.7	95.4	78.1	89.6	75.6
1957 II	67.7	94.8	78.7	89.5	75.7
1957 III	67.8	95.0	79.1	89.7	75.6
1957 IV	67.0	92.8	79.7	88.5	75.6
1958 I	65.3	90.1	79.9	86.8	75.2
1958 II	65.1	89.0	80.3	86.3	75.4
1958 III	66.6	89.8	80.7	87.0	76.5
1958 IV	68.8	91.2	81.1	88.0	78.2

PRIVATE DOMESTIC BUSINESS ECONOMY *(continued)*

OUTPUT, INPUTS, AND PRODUCTIVITY RATIOS
(1967=100)

	REAL OUTPUT	LABOR INPUT	CAPITAL INPUT	TOTAL FACTOR INPUT	TOTAL FACTOR PRODUCTIVITY
1959 I	70.4	92.2	81.6	88.8	79.2
1959 II	72.2	94.4	81.9	90.3	80.0
1959 III	71.1	93.5	82.3	89.9	79.1
1959 IV	71.5	93.2	82.7	89.8	79.6
1960 I	73.4	93.3	83.2	90.1	81.4
1960 II	73.0	93.9	83.5	90.6	80.6
1960 III	72.7	93.9	83.8	90.7	80.1
1960 IV	71.8	92.6	84.1	90.0	79.9
1961 I	72.0	92.0	84.3	89.6	80.3
1961 II	73.2	91.0	84.7	89.1	82.2
1961 III	74.3	91.7	85.1	89.7	82.8
1961 IV	76.4	92.4	85.5	90.3	84.5
1962 I	77.4	93.3	85.9	91.0	85.0
1962 II	78.3	93.7	86.4	91.5	85.6
1962 III	79.1	93.2	86.8	91.4	86.6
1962 IV	79.6	92.7	87.3	91.1	87.4
1963 I	80.5	93.0	87.8	91.5	87.9
1963 II	81.7	93.6	88.2	92.1	88.8
1963 III	82.8	93.7	88.7	92.3	89.8
1963 IV	83.6	94.0	89.2	92.7	90.2
1964 I	84.9	93.9	89.5	92.8	91.5
1964 II	86.1	94.7	90.1	93.5	92.1
1964 III	87.4	95.2	90.7	94.0	93.0
1964 IV	88.4	95.8	91.3	94.6	93.4
1965 I	90.5	96.8	91.8	95.4	94.8
1965 II	92.0	98.1	92.5	96.5	95.3
1965 III	93.2	97.8	93.2	96.6	96.5
1965 IV	95.4	98.8	93.9	97.5	97.9
1966 I	97.0	99.7	94.4	98.2	98.8
1966 II	97.5	100.2	95.3	98.9	98.6
1966 III	98.3	100.2	96.2	99.2	99.1
1966 IV	98.7	100.4	97.2	99.6	99.1
1967 I	98.6	100.3	97.7	99.8	98.8
1967 II	99.4	99.3	98.4	99.4	100.0
1967 III	100.4	99.9	99.2	100.1	100.3
1967 IV	101.6	100.5	100.0	100.7	100.8
1968 I	103.0	100.7	100.6	101.0	101.9
1968 II	104.5	101.3	101.4	101.8	102.7
1968 III	106.3	102.1	102.2	102.5	103.6
1968 IV	107.0	102.8	103.0	103.3	103.6
1969 I	108.0	103.5	103.8	104.1	103.8
1969 II	108.7	104.5	104.7	105.1	103.4
1969 III	108.8	104.9	105.6	105.6	103.0
1969 IV	108.4	104.8	106.5	105.8	102.4

PRIVATE DOMESTIC BUSINESS ECONOMY *(continued)*

OUTPUT, INPUTS, AND PRODUCTIVITY RATIOS
(1967=100)

	REAL OUTPUT	LABOR INPUT	CAPITAL INPUT	TOTAL FACTOR INPUT	TOTAL FACTOR PRODUCTIVITY
1970 I	107.8	103.7	107.1	105.3	102.4
1970 II	107.8	103.2	107.8	105.2	102.5
1970 III	108.6	102.2	108.6	104.8	103.7
1970 IV	107.3	101.4	109.2	104.5	102.7
1971 I	109.6	101.7	109.7	104.8	104.6
1971 II	110.1	102.5	110.5	105.6	104.3
1971 III	111.3	101.9	111.2	105.4	105.6
1971 IV	112.5	103.2	111.8	106.6	105.6
1972 I	115.4	104.7	112.2	107.7	107.2
1972 II	117.3	105.6	113.0	108.5	108.1
1972 III	118.7	106.4	113.9	109.4	108.5
1972 IV	121.3	107.2	114.8	110.2	110.1
1973 I	124.7	108.7	115.5	111.4	111.9
1973 II	124.7	110.0	116.4	112.6	110.7
1973 III	125.1	110.7	117.4	113.4	110.3
1973 IV	125.7	111.1	122.5	115.4	108.9
1974 I	124.3	111.2	110.9	114.2	108.9
1974 II	123.8	111.3	119.7	114.6	108.1
1974 III	122.6	110.9	120.5	114.6	107.0
1974 IV	120.2	109.1	121.3	113.6	105.7
1975 I	116.9	105.5	121.1	111.2	105.2
1975 II	119.2	104.8	121.4	110.8	107.6
1975 III	122.6	105.8	121.9	111.6	109.8
1975 IV	123.7	107.3	122.3	112.8	109.7
1976 I	126.9	108.1	122.5	113.4	112.0
1976 II	128.8	108.8	123.1	114.0	112.9
1976 III	129.8	108.8	123.8	114.3	113.6
1976 IV	130.4	109.3	124.4	114.8	113.6

TOTAL MANUFACTURING

OUTPUT, INPUTS, AND PRODUCTIVITY RATIOS
(1967=100)

	REAL OUTPUT	LABOR INPUT	CAPITAL INPUT	TOTAL FACTOR INPUT	TOTAL FACTOR PRODUCTIVITY
1948	47.8	80.9	54.6	73.7	64.9
1949	45.3	73.7	55.4	68.7	65.9
1950	51.7	79.6	57.5	73.6	70.2
1951	57.5	85.7	62.0	79.3	72.5
1952	59.3	87.0	64.5	80.9	73.4
1953	63.4	91.4	66.7	84.7	75.0
1954	58.9	83.5	67.7	79.3	74.3
1955	65.3	88.1	70.4	83.3	78.3
1956	65.7	89.4	73.8	85.2	77.1
1957	66.1	88.1	75.8	84.8	77.9
1958	60.3	80.9	76.3	79.8	75.7
1959	67.2	86.0	77.7	83.9	80.1
1960	67.7	85.9	78.9	84.1	80.5
1961	67.4	83.5	80.2	82.7	81.5
1962	73.3	86.8	82.1	85.6	85.7
1963	79.1	87.6	83.8	86.6	91.4
1964	84.9	89.2	86.1	88.4	96.1
1965	92.6	94.3	89.5	93.0	99.5
1966	100.0	100.3	95.1	98.9	101.1
1967	100.0	100.0	100.0	100.0	100.0
1968	105.6	101.9	103.9	102.4	103.1
1969	108.7	103.7	107.9	104.8	103.8
1970	102.6	98.2	110.5	101.3	101.3
1971	103.9	94.2	111.6	98.6	105.5
1972	113.6	98.0	113.7	101.9	111.5
1973	123.2	103.2	117.6	106.9	115.3
1974	114.9	101.8	121.9	106.9	107.5
1975	107.6	92.5	121.9	99.8	107.8
1976	120.0	96.6	124.8	103.7	115.8
1977	127.6	100.7	128.4	107.7	118.4
1978P	135.5	104.4	132.2	111.5	121.5

TOTAL MANUFACTURING *(continued)*

OUTPUT, INPUTS, AND PRODUCTIVITY RATIOS
(1967=100)

	REAL OUTPUT	LABOR INPUT	CAPITAL INPUT	TOTAL FACTOR INPUT	TOTAL FACTOR PRODUCTIVITY
1948 I	48.0	81.8	52.5	74.1	64.8
1948 II	47.9	81.1	53.3	73.8	64.9
1948 III	48.0	80.8	53.9	73.8	65.1
1948 IV	47.5	79.5	54.6	73.0	65.1
1949 I	46.3	76.4	54.2	70.6	65.5
1949 II	44.8	73.3	54.7	68.6	65.4
1949 III	45.4	73.0	55.1	68.4	66.3
1949 IV	44.6	71.8	55.4	67.6	66.0
1950 I	46.4	73.9	56.1	69.4	66.9
1950 II	50.1	77.7	56.5	72.2	69.4
1950 III	54.5	82.2	56.9	75.6	72.0
1950 IV	55.7	84.2	57.5	77.3	72.1
1951 I	57.7	86.0	59.9	79.2	72.8
1951 II	58.1	86.9	60.6	80.0	72.6
1951 III	56.9	85.2	61.3	79.0	72.0
1951 IV	57.1	84.7	62.0	78.8	72.5
1952 I	58.3	85.9	62.7	79.9	72.9
1952 II	57.4	85.0	63.4	79.5	72.2
1952 III	58.7	86.1	63.9	80.4	73.0
1952 IV	63.0	90.4	64.5	83.7	75.3
1953 I	64.1	92.4	65.0	85.3	75.2
1953 II	64.6	93.1	65.5	85.9	75.1
1953 III	64.1	91.5	66.1	85.0	75.4
1953 IV	61.0	88.0	66.7	82.5	73.9
1954 I	58.7	85.0	67.2	80.6	72.9
1954 II	58.4	83.2	66.9	79.2	73.8
1954 III	58.4	82.2	67.2	78.5	74.4
1954 IV	60.0	83.4	67.7	79.5	75.5
1955 I	63.0	85.6	68.4	81.3	77.5
1955 II	65.5	87.9	69.0	83.2	78.8
1955 III	65.9	88.5	69.8	83.8	78.6
1955 IV	66.7	90.0	70.4	85.1	78.4
1956 I	66.2	89.7	71.1	85.1	77.8
1956 II	65.6	89.2	72.1	84.9	77.2
1956 III	64.4	88.4	72.9	84.6	76.1
1956 IV	66.7	90.0	73.8	86.0	77.5
1957 I	67.6	89.9	73.8	86.0	78.7
1957 II	66.7	88.8	74.8	85.4	78.1
1957 III	66.6	88.0	75.3	85.0	78.4
1957 IV	63.3	85.2	75.8	83.1	76.2
1958 I	59.3	81.4	75.9	80.4	73.7
1958 II	58.0	78.9	75.8	78.6	73.9
1958 III	60.8	80.5	76.0	79.7	76.2
1958 IV	63.3	82.1	76.3	81.0	78.1

TOTAL MANUFACTURING *(continued)*

OUTPUT, INPUTS, AND PRODUCTIVITY RATIOS
(1967=100)

	REAL OUTPUT	LABOR INPUT	CAPITAL INPUT	TOTAL FACTOR INPUT	TOTAL FACTOR PRODUCTIVITY
1959 I	66.4	84.8	76.3	83.0	80.1
1959 II	69.4	87.2	77.0	84.9	81.8
1959 III	66.5	86.0	77.1	84.1	79.0
1959 IV	66.4	85.7	77.6	84.0	79.1
1960 I	70.5	88.1	77.9	85.8	82.2
1960 II	68.4	86.7	78.5	85.0	80.5
1960 III	67.0	85.3	78.8	84.0	79.7
1960 IV	64.9	82.8	78.9	82.2	79.0
1961 I	63.8	81.5	79.1	81.3	78.4
1961 II	66.4	82.8	79.5	82.3	80.7
1961 III	68.5	83.9	79.8	83.2	82.4
1961 IV	70.9	85.4	80.2	84.4	84.0
1962 I	72.1	85.9	80.7	84.9	84.8
1962 II	72.8	87.2	81.2	86.0	84.6
1962 III	73.7	87.1	81.8	86.1	85.7
1962 IV	74.7	86.7	82.1	85.9	86.9
1963 I	76.4	86.8	82.4	86.0	88.8
1963 II	79.0	87.4	82.7	86.5	91.3
1963 III	79.8	87.7	83.3	87.0	91.8
1963 IV	81.4	87.9	83.8	87.2	93.3
1964 I	82.6	87.9	84.0	87.3	94.7
1964 II	84.5	88.8	84.4	88.0	96.0
1964 III	85.7	89.6	85.1	88.8	96.5
1964 IV	86.8	90.2	86.1	89.5	97.0
1965 I	90.0	92.5	86.6	91.4	98.5
1965 II	91.7	93.3	87.4	92.2	99.5
1965 III	93.5	94.4	88.4	93.3	100.3
1965 IV	95.0	96.2	89.5	94.9	100.2
1966 I	97.8	98.4	90.4	96.8	101.1
1966 II	99.9	100.1	91.7	98.4	101.5
1966 III	100.9	99.8	93.3	98.5	102.4
1966 IV	101.3	101.5	95.0	100.2	101.1
1967 I	99.1	100.5	96.6	99.9	99.1
1967 II	98.9	99.4	97.7	99.4	99.5
1967 III	99.6	99.6	98.8	99.8	99.8
1967 IV	102.4	100.4	100.0	100.8	101.6
1968 I	104.0	100.9	100.7	101.3	102.6
1968 II	105.5	101.5	101.8	102.0	103.4
1968 III	106.0	102.2	102.9	102.9	103.0
1968 IV	107.1	102.9	103.9	103.6	103.4
1969 I	108.6	103.3	104.8	104.2	104.2
1969 II	108.6	103.9	105.9	104.9	103.5
1969 III	109.5	104.3	106.9	105.5	103.8
1969 IV	108.2	103.3	107.9	104.9	103.1

TOTAL MANUFACTURING *(continued)*

OUTPUT, INPUTS, AND PRODUCTIVITY RATIOS
(1967=100)

	REAL OUTPUT	LABOR INPUT	CAPITAL INPUT	TOTAL FACTOR INPUT	TOTAL FACTOR PRODUCTIVITY
1970 I	104.5	100.8	108.6	103.2	101.3
1970 II	103.4	99.3	109.4	102.3	101.1
1970 III	102.6	97.5	109.9	101.1	101.5
1970 IV	99.9	94.0	110.5	98.6	101.3
1971 I	102.3	94.4	110.6	98.9	103.4
1971 II	103.5	94.3	111.2	99.0	104.5
1971 III	103.9	93.6	111.3	98.5	105.4
1971 IV	106.1	94.4	111.5	99.2	107.0
1972 I	109.2	96.0	111.2	100.3	108.9
1972 II	112.1	97.7	111.8	101.8	110.2
1972 III	114.4	98.1	112.9	102.3	111.8
1972 IV	118.8	100.2	113.7	104.1	114.1
1973 I	122.6	102.2	114.4	105.8	115.9
1973 II	124.1	103.4	115.2	106.8	116.1
1973 III	123.9	103.2	116.3	107.0	115.8
1973 IV	122.3	104.3	117.6	108.2	113.0
1974 I	117.0	103.6	118.0	107.7	108.6
1974 II	116.1	102.7	118.9	107.3	108.2
1974 III	116.3	102.5	120.7	107.6	108.1
1974 IV	110.2	98.8	121.9	105.1	104.9
1975 I	101.0	92.3	121.0	100.0	101.0
1975 II	103.8	91.0	121.3	99.0	104.8
1975 III	111.2	92.2	121.5	100.0	111.2
1975 IV	114.3	94.1	121.8	101.5	112.6
1976 I	117.7	96.3	122.0	103.2	114.0
1976 II	119.7	96.6	122.9	103.6	115.5
1976 III	121.0	96.5	123.8	103.8	116.5
1976 IV	121.2	96.9	124.7	104.3	116.2

NONFARM NONMANUFACTURING

OUTPUT, INPUTS, AND PRODUCTIVITY RATIOS
(1967=100)

	REAL OUTPUT	LABOR INPUT	CAPITAL INPUT	TOTAL FACTOR INPUT	TOTAL FACTOR PRODUCTIVITY
1948	47.2	82.9	61.9	74.6	63.2
1949	47.5	81.8	63.4	74.6	63.7
1950	51.2	82.2	65.8	75.8	67.5
1951	53.6	84.6	67.8	78.0	68.7
1952	55.4	85.1	69.1	78.8	70.2
1953	57.2	85.9	70.4	79.8	71.7
1954	58.0	85.5	71.7	80.0	72.5
1955	62.3	88.1	73.8	82.5	75.5
1956	65.2	90.8	76.0	84.9	76.8
1957	66.8	90.6	78.3	85.7	77.9
1958	67.5	88.6	80.0	85.2	79.3
1959	71.9	91.2	81.6	87.4	82.3
1960	73.6	92.2	83.2	88.6	83.1
1961	75.6	90.3	84.8	88.1	85.8
1962	80.0	92.7	86.9	90.4	88.5
1963	82.5	93.6	89.0	91.8	89.9
1964	86.9	95.8	91.4	94.0	92.4
1965	92.4	98.3	94.1	96.6	95.6
1966	97.0	99.9	97.3	98.9	98.1
1967	100.0	100.0	100.0	100.0	100.0
1968	105.3	102.1	103.2	102.6	102.7
1969	108.8	106.3	107.2	106.7	102.0
1970	110.5	107.4	110.4	108.5	101.9
1971	114.2	109.3	113.8	110.9	103.0
1972	120.9	113.2	117.5	114.8	105.3
1973	126.8	117.4	121.4	118.9	106.7
1974	127.2	119.0	124.3	120.9	105.2
1975	127.1	117.0	125.6	120.1	105.8
1976	134.1	120.0	127.8	122.8	109.2
1977	141.0	125.6	131.9	128.0	110.2
1978P	146.6	131.1	136.4	133.1	110.1

NONFARM NONMANUFACTURING *(continued)*

OUTPUT, INPUTS, AND PRODUCTIVITY RATIOS
(1967=100)

	REAL OUTPUT	LABOR INPUT	CAPITAL INPUT	TOTAL FACTOR INPUT	TOTAL FACTOR PRODUCTIVITY
1948 I	46.3	82.4	60.3	74.1	62.5
1948 II	47.3	82.4	60.8	74.3	63.7
1948 III	47.2	83.1	61.4	74.9	63.0
1948 IV	48.1	82.8	61.9	75.0	64.1
1949 I	47.6	82.8	62.2	75.1	63.3
1949 II	47.6	82.3	62.6	74.9	63.5
1949 III	47.8	80.9	63.0	74.2	64.3
1949 IV	47.1	80.8	63.4	74.3	63.4
1950 I	49.3	80.5	64.1	74.4	66.3
1950 II	50.7	81.7	64.6	75.3	67.4
1950 III	52.0	83.1	65.1	76.4	68.1
1950 IV	52.6	83.0	65.8	76.6	68.8
1951 I	52.3	84.3	66.2	77.6	67.5
1951 II	52.7	84.8	66.8	78.0	67.6
1951 III	54.3	84.2	67.3	77.9	69.8
1951 IV	54.9	84.5	67.8	78.3	70.1
1952 I	54.9	84.8	68.1	78.6	69.9
1952 II	55.4	84.5	68.5	78.5	70.5
1952 III	55.1	84.7	68.8	78.8	70.0
1952 IV	56.0	85.9	69.1	79.7	70.3
1953 I	56.8	86.3	69.3	80.0	71.1
1953 II	57.4	86.0	69.6	79.9	71.9
1953 III	57.2	85.4	70.0	79.7	71.8
1953 IV	57.1	85.3	70.4	79.8	71.6
1954 I	57.2	85.1	70.7	79.8	71.6
1954 II	57.1	85.0	71.0	79.8	71.5
1954 III	58.2	85.0	71.4	80.0	72.8
1954 IV	59.5	86.2	71.7	80.9	73.6
1955 I	60.8	87.0	72.2	81.5	74.6
1955 II	61.8	87.2	72.6	81.8	75.5
1955 III	62.9	88.3	73.2	82.7	76.0
1955 IV	63.6	89.4	73.8	83.6	76.1
1956 I	64.0	90.2	74.3	84.3	75.9
1956 II	65.4	90.7	74.9	84.9	77.0
1956 III	65.6	90.7	75.4	85.1	77.1
1956 IV	65.9	90.6	76.0	85.2	77.3
1957 I	66.2	90.6	76.5	85.4	77.5
1957 II	66.7	90.8	77.1	85.8	77.7
1957 III	67.0	90.9	77.6	86.1	77.8
1957 IV	67.1	89.6	78.3	85.5	78.5
1958 I	66.2	88.3	78.5	84.8	78.1
1958 II	66.6	87.4	79.0	84.5	78.8
1958 III	67.5	88.5	79.5	85.3	79.1
1958 IV	69.7	89.6	80.0	86.2	80.9

NONFARM NONMANUFACTURING *(continued)*

OUTPUT, INPUTS, AND PRODUCTIVITY RATIOS
(1967=100)

	REAL OUTPUT	LABOR INPUT	CAPITAL INPUT	TOTAL FACTOR INPUT	TOTAL FACTOR PRODUCTIVITY
1959 I	70.7	90.0	80.6	86.6	81.6
1959 II	72.3	91.0	80.8	87.4	82.8
1959 III	72.2	91.5	81.2	87.8	82.2
1959 IV	72.6	91.5	81.6	88.0	82.5
1960 I	73.5	91.5	82.1	88.2	83.3
1960 II	73.7	92.2	82.4	88.7	83.0
1960 III	73.7	92.3	82.8	88.9	82.9
1960 IV	73.6	91.9	83.2	88.9	82.8
1961 I	74.3	91.7	83.6	88.9	83.6
1961 II	75.0	91.0	84.0	88.6	84.7
1961 III	75.6	91.3	84.4	88.9	85.0
1961 IV	77.6	91.8	84.8	89.4	86.8
1962 I	78.7	92.0	85.4	89.8	87.7
1962 II	79.7	93.0	85.9	90.6	88.0
1962 III	80.5	92.8	86.4	90.7	88.8
1962 IV	81.0	92.2	86.9	90.5	89.5
1963 I	81.2	92.5	87.6	91.0	89.2
1963 II	81.9	93.1	88.1	91.5	89.5
1963 III	83.3	93.5	88.5	91.9	90.6
1963 IV	83.7	94.2	89.0	92.6	90.4
1964 I	85.3	95.1	89.7	93.4	91.4
1964 II	86.2	95.1	90.3	93.6	92.1
1964 III	87.5	95.5	90.8	94.1	93.0
1964 IV	88.5	96.6	91.4	95.0	93.1
1965 I	90.1	97.4	91.9	95.7	94.1
1965 II	91.7	98.4	92.6	96.5	95.0
1965 III	92.4	98.0	93.3	96.6	95.6
1965 IV	95.3	98.5	94.1	97.2	98.1
1966 I	96.3	99.4	94.7	97.9	98.4
1966 II	96.4	99.8	95.6	98.6	97.8
1966 III	97.3	100.4	96.4	99.3	98.0
1966 IV	97.8	99.6	97.3	99.2	98.6
1967 I	98.4	99.7	97.7	99.4	99.0
1967 II	99.7	99.6	98.4	99.6	100.1
1967 III	100.8	100.1	99.2	100.2	100.6
1967 IV	101.1	100.6	100.0	100.8	100.3
1968 I	102.7	100.6	100.7	101.1	101.5
1968 II	104.5	101.7	101.5	102.1	102.4
1968 III	106.7	102.6	102.4	103.0	103.6
1968 IV	107.2	103.5	103.2	103.9	103.2
1969 I	107.8	104.3	104.2	104.7	103.0
1969 II	109.2	106.1	105.2	106.3	102.8
1969 III	109.0	106.9	106.2	107.1	101.7
1969 IV	109.0	107.7	107.2	108.0	101.0

NONFARM NONMANUFACTURING *(continued)*

OUTPUT, INPUTS, AND PRODUCTIVITY RATIOS
(1967=100)

	REAL OUTPUT	LABOR INPUT	CAPITAL INPUT	TOTAL FACTOR INPUT	TOTAL FACTOR PRODUCTIVITY
1970 I	109.6	107.4	107.8	108.1	101.5
1970 II	109.9	107.2	108.7	108.2	101.6
1970 III	111.8	106.9	109.6	108.4	103.2
1970 IV	110.7	107.8	110.4	109.2	101.4
1971 I	112.8	108.1	110.9	109.6	102.9
1971 II	113.3	109.2	111.9	110.7	102.4
1971 III	115.0	108.9	112.9	110.8	103.8
1971 IV	115.7	110.5	113.8	112.2	103.1
1972 I	118.3	112.2	114.4	113.4	104.2
1972 II	120.0	112.9	115.4	114.3	105.0
1972 III	121.9	113.6	116.5	115.1	105.9
1972 IV	123.4	113.9	117.5	115.7	106.7
1973 I	126.4	115.7	118.3	117.1	107.9
1973 II	126.0	117.2	119.3	118.5	106.3
1973 III	126.8	118.3	120.3	119.6	106.1
1973 IV	128.0	118.5	121.4	122.2	104.8
1974 I	129.1	118.4	121.9	120.2	107.4
1974 II	128.1	119.7	122.8	121.3	105.6
1974 III	126.4	119.4	123.5	121.4	104.1
1974 IV	125.4	118.5	124.3	121.0	103.6
1975 I	125.0	116.6	124.2	119.8	104.3
1975 II	126.6	115.9	124.6	119.5	106.0
1975 III	128.3	116.4	125.1	120.0	106.9
1975 IV	128.6	118.4	125.6	121.5	105.8
1976 I	132.1	119.2	125.8	122.1	108.2
1976 II	134.2	119.5	126.5	122.5	109.5
1976 III	135.1	119.7	127.2	122.9	109.9
1976 IV	135.6	120.8	127.8	123.8	109.5

FARMING

OUTPUT, INPUTS, AND PRODUCTIVITY RATIOS
(1967=100)

	REAL OUTPUT	LABOR INPUT	CAPITAL INPUT	TOTAL FACTOR INPUT	TOTAL FACTOR PRODUCTIVITY
1948	86.8	238.6	80.3	169.6	51.2
1949	86.1	236.6	80.8	168.6	51.1
1950	90.9	218.9	83.2	159.5	57.0
1951	87.2	207.4	84.6	153.5	56.8
1952	88.9	197.2	86.0	148.3	59.9
1953	93.2	182.5	86.6	140.1	66.5
1954	95.6	177.3	87.5	137.5	69.5
1955	98.6	180.3	90.0	140.2	70.3
1956	97.3	171.7	90.6	135.5	71.8
1957	94.9	157.9	91.8	128.2	74.1
1958	99.0	146.4	92.6	122.0	81.2
1959	95.3	146.6	94.4	122.8	77.6
1960	99.7	141.4	95.3	120.4	82.8
1961	100.0	133.8	95.4	116.3	86.0
1962	99.7	129.7	96.1	114.4	87.1
1963	101.4	124.3	96.9	111.8	90.7
1964	98.6	117.5	97.9	108.6	90.9
1965	101.7	114.5	98.6	107.2	94.8
1966	96.3	103.7	99.1	101.6	94.8
1967	100.0	100.0	100.0	100.0	100.0
1968	99.3	97.8	100.7	99.2	100.2
1969	101.0	93.1	101.3	96.9	104.3
1970	105.1	86.7	102.3	94.9	110.7
1971	110.8	84.2	103.3	94.5	117.3
1972	108.1	85.1	103.8	95.1	113.6
1973	109.1	83.3	106.0	95.7	114.1
1974	108.8	83.4	106.5	96.0	113.3
1975	114.2	81.0	107.7	95.7	119.3
1976	111.5	77.3	108.0	94.5	118.0
1977	119.1	75.0	110.7	96.0	124.0
1978P	112.5	77.8	111.8	96.8	116.2

FARMING *(continued)*

OUTPUT, INPUTS, AND PRODUCTIVITY RATIOS
(1967=100)

	REAL OUTPUT	LABOR INPUT	CAPITAL INPUT	TOTAL FACTOR INPUT	TOTAL FACTOR PRODUCTIVITY
1948 I	80.1	237.0	75.8	167.2	47.9
1948 II	88.9	233.5	76.9	165.7	53.6
1948 III	85.8	240.1	78.6	170.1	50.4
1948 IV	92.5	242.3	80.3	172.2	53.8
1949 I	83.7	239.6	76.6	169.1	49.5
1949 II	85.0	247.0	78.2	174.0	48.9
1949 III	87.1	236.0	79.4	168.2	51.8
1949 IV	88.8	222.2	80.9	160.9	55.2
1950 I	93.6	218.8	78.4	157.9	59.3
1950 II	90.3	220.3	80.1	159.4	56.6
1950 III	89.0	217.1	81.8	158.3	56.2
1950 IV	90.7	217.7	83.1	159.2	57.0
1951 I	81.9	211.1	81.3	154.7	53.0
1951 II	85.7	205.9	82.3	152.1	56.3
1951 III	91.7	203.5	83.5	151.2	60.7
1951 IV	89.3	207.4	84.6	153.9	58.0
1952 I	86.4	206.4	83.0	152.7	56.6
1952 II	89.3	195.3	84.3	146.8	60.8
1952 III	93.4	192.2	84.8	145.3	64.2
1952 IV	86.3	193.6	86.1	146.6	58.9
1953 I	91.5	189.4	84.3	143.4	63.8
1953 II	93.2	181.8	85.0	139.4	66.9
1953 III	92.6	181.4	85.9	139.6	66.3
1953 IV	95.6	176.0	86.7	136.7	69.9
1954 I	93.9	185.1	85.6	141.6	66.3
1954 II	91.9	176.5	85.9	136.7	67.2
1954 III	98.0	176.3	86.6	136.9	71.6
1954 IV	98.7	170.0	87.5	133.7	73.8
1955 I	96.3	174.1	88.7	136.5	70.6
1955 II	97.4	174.9	89.3	137.2	71.0
1955 III	99.1	184.7	89.7	143.0	69.3
1955 IV	101.8	185.8	90.1	143.8	70.8
1956 I	100.5	172.3	89.9	136.0	73.9
1956 II	93.4	175.4	89.8	137.7	67.8
1956 III	96.8	174.8	90.2	137.6	70.4
1956 IV	98.5	162.4	90.6	130.6	75.4
1957 I	96.3	160.0	91.2	129.5	74.4
1957 II	95.3	155.5	90.9	126.8	75.1
1957 III	93.6	160.3	91.2	129.7	72.2
1957 IV	94.6	154.4	91.8	126.5	74.8
1958 I	99.4	144.7	91.5	120.8	82.3
1958 II	97.7	148.5	92.0	123.2	79.3
1958 III	98.7	144.6	92.2	121.0	81.6
1958 IV	100.1	146.5	92.6	122.3	81.8

FARMING *(continued)*

OUTPUT, INPUTS, AND PRODUCTIVITY RATIOS
(1967=100)

	REAL OUTPUT	LABOR INPUT	CAPITAL INPUT	TOTAL FACTOR INPUT	TOTAL FACTOR PRODUCTIVITY
1959 I	98.0	144.5	93.4	121.4	80.7
1959 II	95.5	155.0	93.8	127.3	75.1
1959 III	91.8	143.9	93.9	121.3	75.7
1959 IV	95.8	141.9	94.4	120.4	79.6
1960 I	95.7	131.8	95.2	115.3	83.0
1960 II	99.7	141.2	95.1	120.4	82.8
1960 III	103.1	147.4	95.2	123.8	83.3
1960 IV	100.2	144.1	95.3	122.1	82.1
1961 I	101.1	143.0	94.6	121.1	83.5
1961 II	99.5	129.0	95.1	113.7	87.5
1961 III	99.2	132.0	95.2	115.4	86.0
1961 IV	100.2	130.2	95.4	114.5	87.5
1962 I	100.4	138.6	94.9	118.9	84.4
1962 II	101.0	130.0	95.3	114.4	88.3
1962 III	99.3	125.4	95.6	112.0	88.7
1962 IV	97.8	124.8	96.1	111.9	87.6
1963 I	101.5	126.3	95.5	112.4	90.2
1963 II	102.5	126.5	96.2	112.9	90.8
1963 III	101.1	122.8	96.5	111.0	91.1
1963 IV	100.3	120.7	96.9	110.0	91.2
1964 I	96.8	113.1	96.0	105.4	91.8
1964 II	97.7	120.1	96.4	109.5	89.2
1964 III	100.0	119.6	97.2	109.6	91.3
1964 IV	100.1	115.3	97.9	107.5	93.1
1965 I	102.0	112.3	98.4	106.2	96.1
1965 II	100.1	118.3	98.4	109.4	91.4
1965 III	104.2	112.1	98.5	106.1	98.2
1965 IV	100.5	113.6	98.6	107.0	93.9
1966 I	102.1	108.1	98.7	104.0	98.2
1966 II	96.4	104.3	98.9	102.0	94.5
1966 III	92.6	100.8	98.9	100.1	92.5
1966 IV	94.0	101.1	99.1	100.3	93.6
1967 I	98.3	103.3	99.3	101.6	96.7
1967 II	97.9	95.7	99.5	97.6	100.3
1967 III	100.9	100.4	99.8	100.3	100.6
1967 IV	103.0	100.6	100.0	100.5	102.4
1968 I	100.3	99.5	100.1	100.0	100.4
1968 II	95.6	97.5	100.3	98.9	96.7
1968 III	100.0	96.5	100.5	98.5	101.6
1968 IV	101.3	96.9	100.7	98.8	102.5
1969 I	105.6	98.0	101.0	98.1	107.7
1969 II	99.5	94.7	101.1	96.9	102.7
1969 III	100.5	91.6	101.2	95.6	105.1
1969 IV	98.5	88.4	101.3	94.5	104.3

FARMING *(continued)*

OUTPUT, INPUTS, AND PRODUCTIVITY RATIOS
(1967=100)

	REAL OUTPUT	LABOR INPUT	CAPITAL INPUT	TOTAL FACTOR INPUT	TOTAL FACTOR PRODUCTIVITY
1970 I	101.7	87.4	101.5	94.1	108.1
1970 II	106.5	89.1	101.8	95.0	112.2
1970 III	102.8	85.9	102.0	93.9	109.5
1970 IV	109.2	84.5	102.3	93.4	116.9
1971 I	115.2	83.0	102.7	93.1	123.7
1971 II	109.0	85.6	102.9	94.3	115.7
1971 III	108.0	84.0	103.1	93.7	115.2
1971 IV	111.0	85.3	103.3	94.4	117.7
1972 I	117.0	85.1	103.4	94.4	124.0
1972 II	114.0	82.7	103.5	93.5	121.9
1972 III	97.5	86.7	103.7	95.1	102.5
1972 IV	104.0	84.6	103.8	94.4	110.1
1973 I	112.5	81.9	104.0	93.4	120.4
1973 II	108.3	82.9	104.7	94.2	114.9
1973 III	103.1	84.0	105.2	95.0	108.5
1973 IV	112.6	83.5	106.0	95.2	118.3
1974 I	102.2	87.9	106.1	97.0	105.3
1974 II	113.0	83.6	106.3	95.4	118.4
1974 III	108.9	80.4	106.4	94.2	115.6
1974 IV	111.0	81.1	106.5	94.6	117.3
1975 I	107.5	77.5	106.8	93.3	115.2
1975 II	116.0	79.7	107.1	94.3	122.9
1975 III	117.0	83.5	107.3	96.0	121.8
1975 IV	116.3	79.0	107.7	94.4	123.1
1976 I	112.6	73.2	107.8	92.2	122.1
1976 II	109.1	79.1	107.8	94.5	115.4
1976 III	108.8	78.1	108.0	94.2	115.4
1976 IV	115.2	74.7	108.0	92.9	124.0

MINING

OUTPUT, INPUTS, AND PRODUCTIVITY RATIOS
(1967=100)

	REAL OUTPUT	LABOR INPUT	CAPITAL INPUT	TOTAL FACTOR INPUT	TOTAL FACTOR PRODUCTIVITY
1948	67.9	148.0	96.8	125.8	54.0
1949	59.8	128.5	95.5	114.2	52.3
1950	66.9	130.2	99.8	117.0	57.1
1951	73.1	136.2	99.7	120.4	60.8
1952	72.2	132.7	98.1	117.7	61.4
1953	73.9	129.5	89.5	112.2	65.9
1954	71.7	118.7	90.6	106.6	67.2
1955	79.8	125.6	96.3	112.9	70.6
1956	84.1	131.4	95.5	115.8	72.6
1957	83.9	130.0	99.4	116.8	71.9
1958	77.3	114.4	102.3	109.2	70.8
1959	80.8	115.6	108.2	112.5	71.8
1960	81.9	112.6	111.2	112.0	73.2
1961	82.5	105.2	117.1	110.3	74.8
1962	84.9	104.2	117.8	110.0	77.2
1963	88.5	101.4	104.1	102.6	86.3
1964	90.8	102.3	102.6	102.4	88.6
1965	93.7	101.9	96.7	99.7	94.0
1966	98.2	102.1	102.5	102.3	96.1
1967	100.0	100.0	100.0	100.0	100.0
1968	103.3	100.7	102.8	101.6	101.7
1969	106.5	100.6	111.9	105.4	101.0
1970	108.9	102.6	111.8	106.6	102.2
1971	106.0	100.7	112.5	105.7	100.3
1972	108.1	104.0	114.0	108.3	99.8
1973	109.4	107.7	116.0	111.3	98.3
1974	108.7	116.5	117.0	117.0	92.9
1975	108.2	125.7	117.7	122.7	88.2
1976	109.7	135.0	118.4	128.5	85.4
1973 I	110.2	103.3	114.4	107.6	102.4
1973 II	110.0	105.4	115.0	109.1	100.8
1973 III	110.0	107.6	115.6	110.7	99.4
1973 IV	107.6	113.0	116.0	114.0	94.4
1974 I	107.0	114.2	116.1	114.8	93.2
1974 II	102.6	117.8	116.5	117.1	87.6
1974 III	112.1	117.9	116.5	117.1	95.7
1974 IV	113.0	114.2	117.0	115.2	98.1
1975 I	111.2	121.0	116.8	119.1	93.4
1975 II	110.2	122.7	117.1	120.2	91.7
1975 III	104.4	124.6	117.1	121.4	86.0
1975 IV	106.9	128.9	117.7	124.2	86.1
1976 I	106.9	132.8	117.9	126.5	84.5
1976 II	107.1	131.7	118.0	125.9	85.0
1976 III	107.6	132.0	118.3	126.2	85.3
1976 IV	109.6	137.2	118.5	129.4	84.7

CONTRACT CONSTRUCTION

OUTPUT, INPUTS, AND PRODUCTIVITY RATIOS
(1967=100)

	REAL OUTPUT	LABOR INPUT	CAPITAL INPUT	TOTAL FACTOR INPUT	TOTAL FACTOR PRODUCTIVITY
1948	44.6	75.0	31.1	72.1	61.8
1949	44.5	74.5	32.8	71.8	62.1
1950	49.1	77.9	36.7	75.2	65.2
1951	54.6	85.8	41.6	82.9	65.9
1952	56.9	87.9	44.7	85.1	66.9
1953	58.7	86.3	45.8	83.6	70.1
1954	60.4	85.0	47.3	82.5	73.2
1955	64.1	90.1	48.7	87.3	73.4
1956	68.7	96.6	51.8	93.7	73.3
1957	68.8	93.7	55.9	91.3	75.4
1958	70.8	89.7	58.7	87.7	80.8
1959	76.2	94.4	62.6	92.3	82.6
1960	77.3	92.4	65.9	90.6	85.3
1961	78.2	89.6	70.3	88.3	88.5
1962	81.0	92.6	74.9	91.5	88.6
1963	83.5	94.9	80.8	94.0	88.8
1964	90.1	97.4	85.7	96.6	93.3
1965	95.6	100.3	91.0	99.7	95.8
1966	99.2	103.5	95.1	103.0	96.3
1967	100.0	100.0	100.0	100.0	100.0
1968	104.9	101.4	103.5	101.5	103.3
1969	102.5	107.3	109.9	107.5	95.4
1970	95.4	108.2	113.7	108.6	87.8
1971	95.2	112.6	117.4	112.9	84.3
1972	96.1	118.1	122.5	118.4	81.2
1973	96.8	124.8	125.4	124.8	77.5
1974	92.9	124.8	126.9	124.9	74.3
1975	83.8	113.0	123.8	113.8	73.6
1976	91.6	111.5	121.7	112.2	81.6
1973 I	97.9	118.4	123.1	118.7	82.4
1973 II	94.6	124.7	123.8	124.7	75.9
1973 III	96.2	127.1	124.6	127.0	75.8
1973 IV	98.3	126.9	398.8	147.0	66.9
1974 I	97.6	125.6	125.6	125.6	77.7
1974 II	97.0	126.4	126.2	126.4	76.8
1974 III	86.6	124.3	126.3	124.4	69.6
1974 IV	90.2	122.0	126.9	122.4	73.7
1975 I	88.8	111.3	125.6	112.4	79.0
1975 II	95.3	109.2	124.6	110.3	86.4
1975 III	75.7	113.1	124.2	113.9	66.4
1975 IV	75.3	112.6	123.8	113.5	66.4
1976 I	82.7	103.7	123.4	105.2	78.6
1976 II	83.8	110.2	122.8	111.2	75.4
1976 III	81.6	112.0	122.0	112.8	72.4
1976 IV	88.2	114.8	121.7	115.3	76.5

TOTAL TRANSPORTATION

OUTPUT, INPUTS, AND PRODUCTIVITY RATIOS
(1967=100)

	REAL OUTPUT	LABOR INPUT	CAPITAL INPUT	TOTAL FACTOR INPUT	TOTAL FACTOR PRODUCTIVITY
1947	66.6	116.2	81.3	109.3	60.9
1948	58.5	106.6	83.5	102.0	57.4
1949	64.5	105.8	86.3	101.9	63.3
1950	71.5	110.7	88.8	106.4	67.2
1951	69.3	108.4	90.7	104.9	66.1
1952	69.9	108.3	92.3	105.2	66.5
1953	66.6	101.4	94.4	100.0	66.6
1954	72.6	104.4	96.5	102.8	70.5
1955	76.4	105.8	98.2	104.3	73.2
1956	75.6	103.0	99.5	102.3	73.9
1957	70.5	94.1	100.1	95.3	74.0
1958	74.3	96.2	99.6	96.8	76.7
1959	75.8	95.3	98.2	95.9	79.1
1960	75.1	91.1	97.5	92.3	81.4
1961	78.4	92.7	97.8	93.7	83.7
1962	82.6	92.3	98.2	93.4	88.4
1963	85.5	93.5	98.3	94.4	90.6
1964	93.2	96.3	98.7	96.8	96.4
1965	100.4	98.9	99.5	99.0	101.4
1966	100.0	100.0	100.0	100.0	100.0
1967	106.7	102.2	100.4	101.8	104.8
1968	108.4	101.2	100.9	101.1	107.2
1969	107.6	102.4	101.1	102.1	105.3
1970	106.6	100.9	100.8	100.9	105.6
1971	113.6	103.6	100.7	103.0	110.3
1972	124.2	107.2	100.5	105.9	117.3
1973	123.9	106.7	100.3	105.5	117.5
1974	114.6	99.9	100.0	99.9	114.7
1975	120.5	102.3	99.6	101.8	118.3
1973 I	114.6	104.6	100.7	103.8	110.4
1973 II	116.8	107.1	100.7	105.9	110.3
1973 III	135.4	107.0	100.6	105.8	127.9
1973 IV	130.0	108.7	100.5	107.1	121.3
1974 I	120.1	106.0	100.5	105.0	114.4
1974 II	119.9	107.4	100.4	106.1	113.0
1974 III	128.4	106.2	100.4	105.1	122.2
1974 IV	127.2	106.2	100.3	105.1	121.1
1975 I	116.6	99.4	100.3	99.6	117.1
1975 II	124.4	98.3	100.2	98.7	126.1
1975 III	111.2	98.7	100.1	99.0	112.3
1975 IV	106.3	100.0	100.0	100.1	106.2
1976 I	109.7	101.0	99.9	100.8	108.8
1976 II	115.0	100.9	99.8	100.7	114.2
1976 III	118.5	101.9	99.7	101.5	116.7
1976 IV	113.7	102.4	99.6	101.9	111.6

RAILROAD TRANSPORTATION

OUTPUT, INPUTS, AND PRODUCTIVITY RATIOS
(1967=100)

	REAL OUTPUT	LABOR INPUT	CAPITAL INPUT	TOTAL FACTOR INPUT	TOTAL FACTOR PRODUCTIVITY
1948	96.8	230.5	96.8	201.5	48.1
1949	80.4	197.3	97.9	175.7	45.8
1950	87.4	187.8	99.5	168.6	51.8
1951	98.3	197.3	101.0	176.4	55.7
1952	94.1	189.3	102.2	170.4	55.2
1953	91.6	187.0	103.5	168.9	54.3
1954	82.7	166.4	105.2	153.1	54.0
1955	91.5	170.1	106.5	156.3	58.6
1956	93.7	168.0	107.1	154.8	60.5
1957	88.2	158.0	107.4	147.0	60.0
1958	78.5	134.0	107.5	128.3	61.2
1959	82.0	129.4	106.9	124.6	65.8
1960	81.1	123.5	105.4	119.6	67.8
1961	80.4	113.6	104.0	111.6	72.1
1962	83.4	113.1	102.9	110.9	75.2
1963	87.6	109.9	101.8	108.2	81.0
1964	91.3	109.0	101.2	107.3	85.1
1965	98.7	106.2	100.7	105.0	94.0
1966	105.6	105.0	100.5	104.0	101.5
1967	100.0	100.0	100.0	100.0	100.0
1968	98.3	99.6	99.2	99.5	98.8
1969	100.9	94.7	98.7	95.6	105.6
1970	95.5	94.9	98.0	95.6	99.9
1971	85.7	89.4	97.2	91.0	94.2
1972	86.5	87.5	96.5	89.3	96.8
1973	95.8	88.5	95.7	90.0	106.5
1974	92.0	89.8	95.2	90.9	101.2
1975	79.4	82.6	94.4	85.0	93.4
1976	79.7	81.1	93.6	83.6	95.3
1973 I	86.3	87.7	96.4	89.4	96.6
1973 II	86.2	88.9	96.2	90.3	95.4
1973 III	107.1	87.4	96.0	89.1	120.3
1973 IV	103.7	88.5	95.7	89.9	115.3
1974 I	86.8	89.0	95.6	90.3	96.2
1974 II	87.6	90.2	95.5	91.2	96.1
1974 III	93.5	89.4	95.3	90.6	103.2
1974 IV	100.0	89.1	95.2	90.3	110.8
1975 I	87.1	85.5	95.0	87.4	99.7
1975 II	94.2	80.8	94.8	83.5	112.8
1975 III	66.2	79.6	94.6	82.5	80.3
1975 IV	70.1	80.1	94.4	82.9	84.5
1976 I	71.1	80.4	94.2	83.1	85.6
1976 II	74.9	81.5	94.0	83.9	89.2
1976 III	72.5	81.9	93.8	84.2	86.1
1976 IV	74.9	81.7	93.6	84.0	89.2

NONRAIL TRANSPORTATION

OUTPUT, INPUTS, AND PRODUCTIVITY RATIOS
(1967=100)

	REAL OUTPUT	LABOR INPUT	CAPITAL INPUT	TOTAL FACTOR INPUT	TOTAL FACTOR PRODUCTIVITY
1948	54.1	78.6	37.8	71.2	75.9
1949	49.5	76.8	43.0	70.7	70.0
1950	55.0	78.8	49.2	73.4	74.9
1951	60.4	82.2	54.8	77.2	78.3
1952	59.0	81.8	58.5	77.5	76.1
1953	60.9	82.5	61.0	78.6	77.5
1954	60.0	80.0	64.0	77.1	77.8
1955	64.7	82.8	68.4	80.2	80.7
1956	69.2	85.3	73.2	83.1	83.3
1957	70.3	84.9	77.4	83.5	84.2
1958	67.2	81.0	79.6	80.7	83.3
1959	71.1	85.2	79.0	84.1	84.6
1960	73.6	86.0	78.1	84.5	87.1
1961	72.9	83.7	79.4	82.9	88.0
1962	76.4	86.0	83.4	85.5	89.3
1963	80.5	86.5	88.0	86.8	92.8
1964	83.1	88.4	90.2	88.7	93.6
1965	91.0	93.0	93.1	93.0	97.8
1966	98.2	96.9	96.5	96.8	101.4
1967	100.0	100.0	100.0	100.0	100.0
1968	110.2	103.0	103.7	103.1	106.9
1969	111.5	103.3	107.0	104.0	107.2
1970	112.6	104.8	109.7	105.7	106.4
1971	115.2	104.7	110.6	105.8	108.8
1972	124.8	108.8	112.5	109.5	114.0
1973	136.0	113.3	113.9	113.4	119.9
1974	137.2	112.2	114.8	112.7	121.7
1975	129.2	105.6	115.7	107.5	120.3
1976	137.4	109.3	116.2	110.6	124.2
1973 I	126.3	110.1	112.7	110.9	113.9
1973 II	129.5	113.1	113.3	113.4	114.2
1973 III	147.1	113.5	113.7	113.9	129.2
1973 IV	140.9	115.3	113.9	115.3	122.1
1974 I	134.0	111.7	114.1	112.4	119.1
1974 II	133.3	113.1	114.4	113.7	117.3
1974 III	142.8	111.7	114.6	112.5	126.9
1974 IV	138.5	111.8	114.8	112.7	122.9
1975 I	128.9	104.0	115.1	106.4	121.1
1975 II	137.0	104.1	115.5	106.6	128.5
1975 III	129.8	105.0	115.5	107.3	121.0
1975 IV	121.3	106.6	115.7	108.6	111.7
1976 I	125.7	107.7	115.7	109.6	114.7
1976 II	131.6	107.3	116.1	109.2	120.5
1976 III	137.5	108.4	116.1	110.2	124.8
1976 IV	129.8	109.2	116.2	110.8	117.1

COMMUNICATIONS

OUTPUT, INPUTS, AND PRODUCTIVITY RATIOS
(1967=100)

	REAL OUTPUT	LABOR INPUT	CAPITAL INPUT	TOTAL FACTOR INPUT	TOTAL FACTOR PRODUCTIVITY
1948	28.8	90.6	34.9	68.3	42.2
1949	30.3	87.7	36.3	67.0	45.1
1950	31.7	84.5	37.9	65.6	48.3
1951	35.0	86.7	39.9	67.6	51.8
1952	37.1	88.7	42.7	69.8	53.1
1953	40.7	92.2	45.1	72.9	55.8
1954	41.5	91.1	47.5	73.0	56.8
1955	45.6	91.5	49.6	74.0	61.7
1956	48.4	94.6	53.1	77.1	62.8
1957	51.9	93.7	57.1	77.9	66.5
1958	53.7	87.8	60.0	75.2	71.4
1959	57.7	86.4	62.5	75.2	76.7
1960	61.1	87.5	65.8	77.4	78.9
1961	63.9	84.4	69.5	77.5	82.5
1962	68.6	86.1	73.1	80.1	85.7
1963	73.6	86.0	76.9	81.8	90.0
1964	78.4	88.6	81.8	85.4	91.8
1965	85.2	92.8	87.5	90.3	94.4
1966	93.1	97.9	93.7	96.0	97.0
1967	100.0	100.0	100.0	100.0	100.0
1968	106.9	104.7	106.1	105.4	101.5
1969	119.5	109.9	113.1	111.4	107.3
1970	128.9	118.7	121.7	120.1	107.3
1971	134.8	116.7	130.0	122.8	109.8
1972	147.7	122.9	138.3	130.0	113.7
1973	161.1	126.7	147.0	136.0	118.4
1974	169.1	129.2	155.9	141.5	119.5
1975	183.5	127.9	161.9	143.5	127.8
1976	196.7	127.9	167.9	146.3	134.4
1973 I	153.7	123.8	140.5	132.9	115.6
1973 II	155.5	125.3	142.6	134.7	115.4
1973 III	168.3	127.6	144.8	137.0	122.9
1973 IV	166.9	127.9	147.0	138.2	120.8
1974 I	164.6	127.7	149.5	139.2	118.2
1974 II	165.7	130.1	151.7	141.6	117.0
1974 III	174.4	129.8	153.9	142.4	122.5
1974 IV	171.7	127.2	155.9	141.9	121.0
1975 I	173.5	124.1	157.7	141.0	123.0
1975 II	172.2	123.2	159.1	141.2	121.9
1975 III	194.8	123.9	160.4	142.2	137.0
1975 IV	193.4	123.1	161.9	142.5	135.7
1976 I	191.4	125.6	163.3	144.5	132.5
1976 II	196.8	123.1	164.7	143.7	136.9
1976 III	200.5	125.1	166.2	145.5	137.8
1976 IV	201.9	124.3	167.9	145.9	138.4

PUBLIC UTILITIES

OUTPUT, INPUTS, AND PRODUCTIVITY RATIOS
(1967=100)

	REAL OUTPUT	LABOR INPUT	CAPITAL INPUT	TOTAL FACTOR INPUT	TOTAL FACTOR PRODUCTIVITY
1948	27.1	90.4	46.2	65.2	41.6
1949	30.0	91.2	48.6	66.9	44.9
1950	32.2	91.6	51.5	68.7	46.9
1951	37.3	91.8	54.8	70.6	52.8
1952	40.0	91.6	57.7	72.1	55.4
1953	43.0	92.6	61.3	74.5	57.7
1954	47.1	92.6	64.0	76.0	62.0
1955	49.8	93.4	66.9	78.0	63.9
1956	53.5	93.5	69.5	79.4	67.3
1957	56.6	94.2	73.2	81.7	69.3
1958	58.9	93.5	77.4	83.8	70.3
1959	64.3	93.4	79.4	84.8	75.8
1960	69.0	94.0	82.7	87.1	79.2
1961	72.7	92.0	84.4	87.4	83.2
1962	76.0	92.9	85.8	88.5	85.8
1963	79.9	94.0	87.6	90.1	88.7
1964	85.2	93.8	89.9	91.4	93.2
1965	89.4	96.2	92.5	94.0	95.1
1966	95.1	97.6	95.9	96.6	98.5
1967	100.0	100.0	100.0	100.0	100.0
1968	108.2	103.9	104.7	104.4	103.7
1969	114.9	104.3	110.0	107.8	106.6
1970	118.1	110.2	115.6	113.5	104.1
1971	124.8	110.4	121.9	117.4	106.3
1972	128.8	113.3	128.7	122.7	105.0
1973	137.7	116.6	135.8	128.3	107.4
1974	130.1	118.2	142.4	132.9	97.9
1975	135.9	116.3	147.0	134.9	100.8
1976	132.0	117.0	151.7	138.0	95.6
1973 I	132.0	115.3	130.5	125.8	104.9
1973 II	132.8	116.1	132.2	127.1	104.5
1973 III	143.2	116.6	133.9	128.4	111.5
1973 IV	142.8	116.1	135.8	129.3	110.4
1974 I	134.8	117.8	137.6	131.1	102.8
1974 II	139.3	118.6	139.2	132.4	105.2
1974 III	121.8	117.2	140.8	132.8	91.7
1974 IV	124.4	117.1	142.4	133.8	93.0
1975 I	133.9	116.9	143.7	134.4	99.6
1975 II	131.8	116.3	144.8	134.9	97.7
1975 III	137.5	114.8	145.9	135.0	101.9
1975 IV	140.5	115.5	147.0	135.9	103.4
1976 I	135.6	120.0	148.1	138.4	98.0
1976 II	132.9	117.8	149.3	138.2	96.2
1976 III	132.1	117.6	150.4	138.8	95.2
1976 IV	134.8	117.0	151.7	139.4	96.7

TRADE

OUTPUT, INPUTS, AND PRODUCTIVITY RATIOS
(1967=100)

	REAL OUTPUT	LABOR INPUT	CAPITAL INPUT	TOTAL FACTOR INPUT	TOTAL FACTOR PRODUCTIVITY
1948	48.6	82.6	49.9	77.1	63.0
1949	49.7	83.4	52.4	78.2	63.6
1950	54.5	83.9	57.8	79.6	68.4
1951	55.0	85.8	61.3	81.8	67.2
1952	56.6	86.0	63.1	82.3	68.8
1953	58.5	87.2	64.2	83.5	70.1
1954	58.9	87.9	64.7	84.1	70.0
1955	64.2	90.4	68.0	86.8	74.0
1956	66.1	93.0	71.1	89.5	73.9
1957	67.2	92.7	73.9	89.8	74.8
1958	67.1	91.5	74.9	89.0	75.4
1959	72.0	94.1	76.9	91.4	78.8
1960	73.4	95.5	78.7	92.9	79.0
1961	74.1	93.2	79.3	91.1	81.4
1962	78.8	95.1	81.7	93.1	84.7
1963	82.0	94.3	84.9	92.9	88.3
1964	86.9	97.0	87.8	95.6	90.9
1965	92.5	99.5	91.9	98.4	94.1
1966	97.6	100.4	97.1	99.9	97.7
1967	100.0	100.0	100.0	100.0	100.0
1968	106.1	101.8	103.2	102.0	104.1
1969	108.6	108.1	106.6	107.8	100.7
1970	111.0	106.6	109.2	107.0	103.7
1971	116.2	109.4	113.7	110.1	105.6
1972	125.2	112.7	118.1	113.5	110.3
1973	131.8	115.8	123.2	116.9	112.7
1974	128.0	116.3	126.1	117.9	108.6
1975	129.7	116.7	123.7	117.8	110.1
1976	136.5	120.1	127.2	121.2	112.6
1973 I	130.3	114.9	119.4	115.8	112.6
1973 II	127.0	115.3	120.4	116.4	109.1
1973 III	133.7	115.7	121.3	116.8	114.5
1973 IV	136.2	115.7	123.2	117.1	116.3
1974 I	132.4	115.3	124.0	116.8	113.4
1974 II	132.4	116.6	124.8	118.1	112.1
1974 III	125.3	116.5	125.3	118.1	106.1
1974 IV	121.7	115.6	126.1	117.4	103.6
1975 I	130.0	114.7	124.5	116.4	111.6
1975 II	130.7	114.5	123.4	116.1	112.5
1975 III	130.0	113.6	124.1	115.4	112.6
1975 IV	128.2	118.2	123.7	119.3	107.5
1976 I	131.5	119.0	125.0	120.2	109.4
1976 II	132.7	118.2	126.0	119.7	110.9
1976 III	134.1	117.3	127.1	119.0	112.7
1976 IV	135.7	120.2	127.3	121.5	111.7

FINANCE AND INSURANCE

OUTPUT, INPUTS, AND PRODUCTIVITY RATIOS
(1967=100)

	REAL OUTPUT	LABOR INPUT	CAPITAL INPUT	TOTAL FACTOR INPUT	TOTAL FACTOR PRODUCTIVITY
1948	50.5	58.4	37.0	54.3	93.1
1949	52.9	59.4	37.8	55.2	95.8
1950	55.0	61.0	39.1	56.8	96.8
1951	57.2	63.1	40.3	58.8	97.4
1952	60.4	65.6	42.9	61.2	98.6
1953	63.2	68.1	47.1	64.1	98.6
1954	66.2	70.8	47.5	66.3	99.8
1955	70.6	74.1	51.3	69.7	101.3
1956	74.2	75.9	54.6	71.8	103.2
1957	77.3	76.9	57.6	73.3	105.6
1958	78.0	78.6	60.5	75.2	103.6
1959	78.2	80.8	64.3	77.7	100.6
1960	81.4	83.7	67.6	80.7	100.9
1961	85.0	83.9	71.8	81.7	104.1
1962	95.1	87.7	76.1	85.5	111.3
1963	87.6	89.1	80.7	87.5	100.1
1964	87.6	91.9	84.9	90.6	96.6
1965	95.2	94.2	89.5	93.4	102.0
1966	95.6	95.9	94.1	95.5	100.1
1967	100.0	100.0	100.0	100.0	100.0
1968	106.9	106.7	105.5	106.5	100.4
1969	113.0	109.4	112.3	109.9	102.8
1970	117.4	114.5	119.0	115.2	101.9
1971	118.4	118.0	127.0	119.1	99.4
1972	122.3	122.3	134.6	123.8	98.8
1973	121.3	127.1	142.1	128.9	94.1
1974	131.2	131.1	149.3	133.2	98.5
1975	133.9	133.6	156.8	136.2	98.3
1976	136.4	138.6	163.8	141.4	96.5
1973 I	123.3	125.6	136.7	127.1	97.0
1973 II	126.5	126.1	138.4	127.7	99.1
1973 III	112.3	126.5	140.5	128.3	87.5
1973 IV	122.9	127.8	142.1	129.6	94.8
1974 I	122.5	130.0	144.2	131.8	92.9
1974 II	118.5	130.4	145.9	132.4	89.5
1974 III	133.9	129.3	147.6	131.6	101.8
1974 IV	149.8	131.5	149.3	133.7	112.0
1975 I	129.8	133.3	151.0	135.5	95.8
1975 II	131.7	131.7	152.6	134.2	98.1
1975 III	132.5	131.0	154.7	133.7	99.1
1975 IV	141.6	133.0	156.8	135.8	104.3
1976 I	136.0	138.3	158.6	140.7	96.6
1976 II	133.9	136.4	160.3	139.2	96.1
1976 III	133.9	136.2	162.1	139.2	96.2
1976 IV	144.8	136.7	163.8	139.8	103.6

REAL ESTATE

OUTPUT, INPUTS, AND PRODUCTIVITY RATIOS
(1967=100)

	REAL OUTPUT	LABOR INPUT	CAPITAL INPUT	TOTAL FACTOR INPUT	TOTAL FACTOR PRODUCTIVITY
1948	38.8	71.4	71.8	71.6	54.1
1949	41.4	72.7	72.5	72.4	57.3
1950	44.5	73.8	73.7	73.5	60.5
1951	45.9	75.1	74.7	74.6	61.6
1952	49.2	76.7	75.1	75.1	65.5
1953	51.1	79.4	75.8	76.0	67.2
1954	53.6	82.3	76.9	77.2	69.4
1955	56.3	85.5	77.9	78.4	71.8
1956	58.8	87.1	79.6	80.1	73.4
1957	61.6	88.7	81.1	81.6	75.5
1958	65.2	90.6	82.1	82.7	78.8
1959	69.7	92.5	83.4	84.1	82.9
1960	72.2	92.5	84.8	85.4	84.5
1961	75.8	90.2	86.5	86.7	87.4
1962	80.7	93.5	88.6	88.9	90.7
1963	83.3	101.0	91.0	91.7	90.8
1964	87.3	102.1	93.4	94.0	92.8
1965	92.5	102.0	95.9	96.3	96.0
1966	96.5	98.7	98.0	98.1	98.4
1967	100.0	100.0	100.0	100.0	100.0
1968	104.0	102.9	102.5	102.5	101.5
1969	108.3	107.1	105.7	105.8	102.3
1970	110.1	112.2	108.5	108.7	101.3
1971	117.7	122.0	111.2	112.0	105.1
1972	123.2	130.6	114.3	115.6	106.6
1973	127.6	135.2	117.4	118.8	107.5
1974	133.0	137.5	119.1	120.5	110.4
1975	134.3	136.3	120.2	121.4	110.6
1976	144.7	140.9	121.3	122.8	117.9
1973 I	129.4	120.6	114.4	116.8	110.8
1973 II	128.3	124.5	115.5	118.1	108.6
1973 III	126.8	126.5	116.5	119.2	106.3
1973 IV	126.2	125.0	117.4	120.0	105.2
1974 I	133.3	124.2	116.9	119.5	111.6
1974 II	132.8	128.0	117.8	120.5	110.2
1974 III	134.4	127.3	118.5	121.2	110.9
1974 IV	131.6	125.5	119.1	121.6	108.2
1975 I	128.5	123.1	118.5	120.8	106.3
1975 II	134.1	124.7	119.0	121.5	110.3
1975 III	138.0	125.4	119.6	122.1	113.0
1975 IV	136.8	124.9	120.2	122.6	111.7
1976 I	135.8	127.4	119.3	121.9	111.4
1976 II	137.1	128.2	119.9	122.6	111.9
1976 III	141.6	129.7	120.6	123.3	114.8
1976 IV	149.8	128.6	121.3	123.9	120.9

SERVICES

OUTPUT, INPUTS, AND PRODUCTIVITY RATIOS
(1967=100)

	REAL OUTPUT	LABOR INPUT	CAPITAL INPUT	TOTAL FACTOR INPUT	TOTAL FACTOR PRODUCTIVITY
1948	51.4	75.8	49.7	70.0	73.3
1949	51.2	75.2	50.4	69.7	73.5
1950	52.7	74.3	51.3	69.1	76.3
1951	53.8	73.9	52.2	69.0	77.9
1952	55.2	74.9	52.3	69.8	79.0
1953	56.1	75.4	52.6	70.3	79.8
1954	56.1	75.5	53.0	70.5	79.6
1955	59.2	77.0	54.4	71.9	82.2
1956	62.4	78.6	56.7	73.7	84.7
1957	64.4	80.5	59.2	75.7	85.1
1958	66.2	80.7	61.4	76.3	86.8
1959	71.1	83.4	64.2	79.0	90.0
1960	71.1	85.8	67.4	81.5	87.2
1961	74.7	85.9	70.8	82.4	90.7
1962	77.4	89.3	75.0	86.0	90.0
1963	81.1	93.0	79.7	90.0	90.2
1964	86.0	94.5	84.2	92.2	93.3
1965	90.0	97.0	89.5	95.3	94.4
1966	94.6	99.3	95.4	98.4	96.1
1967	100.0	100.0	100.0	100.0	100.0
1968	103.2	101.2	107.2	102.6	100.6
1969	108.8	103.6	114.8	106.1	102.5
1970	113.4	106.5	119.0	109.3	103.8
1971	115.5	106.2	122.9	109.8	105.2
1972	124.9	110.5	127.4	114.2	109.4
1973	134.1	115.9	132.3	119.6	112.1
1974	136.9	119.5	136.5	123.3	111.1
1975	136.1	117.0	139.3	121.7	111.8
1976	143.7	120.5	142.3	125.2	114.8
1973 I	130.3	116.0	128.5	119.2	109.3
1973 II	128.5	116.8	129.9	120.1	107.1
1973 III	138.5	119.2	131.3	122.3	113.3
1973 IV	139.0	118.3	132.3	121.8	114.1
1974 I	137.7	119.9	133.6	123.3	111.7
1974 II	135.1	121.2	134.7	124.5	108.5
1974 III	135.9	122.3	135.8	125.7	108.1
1974 IV	138.9	120.8	136.5	124.6	111.5
1975 I	138.7	121.3	137.1	125.1	110.8
1975 II	140.7	120.3	137.8	124.4	113.1
1975 III	133.7	122.6	138.5	126.5	105.8
1975 IV	131.2	121.3	139.3	125.5	104.5
1976 I	142.4	124.4	140.0	128.2	111.1
1976 II	146.9	125.2	140.8	129.0	113.9
1976 III	143.3	126.5	141.5	130.1	110.1
1976 IV	124.2	123.7	142.3	128.0	97.0

FOOD

OUTPUT, INPUTS, AND PRODUCTIVITY RATIOS
(1967=100)

	REAL OUTPUT	LABOR INPUT	CAPITAL INPUT	TOTAL FACTOR INPUT	TOTAL FACTOR PRODUCTIVITY
1948	59.3	106.5	85.5	100.5	59.0
1949	57.9	104.2	88.9	99.8	58.0
1950	61.8	104.0	91.5	100.4	61.5
1951	62.6	105.8	94.0	102.5	61.0
1952	66.1	104.8	92.9	101.5	65.1
1953	70.0	104.3	91.8	100.8	69.5
1954	69.2	103.2	91.5	99.9	69.3
1955	70.8	103.7	94.6	101.1	70.0
1956	74.0	104.2	95.5	101.8	72.7
1957	76.6	101.3	95.6	99.8	76.8
1958	77.1	99.5	96.6	98.8	78.1
1959	78.5	101.0	96.3	99.7	78.7
1960	79.1	101.2	95.1	99.6	79.4
1961	80.1	100.3	95.4	99.0	80.9
1962	83.1	99.0	96.4	98.3	84.5
1963	88.9	98.4	96.5	97.9	90.8
1964	91.0	98.1	97.3	97.9	92.9
1965	93.1	99.0	95.6	98.1	94.9
1966	99.6	99.5	97.4	98.9	100.7
1967	100.0	100.0	100.0	100.0	100.0
1968	101.2	99.5	101.2	100.0	101.2
1969	104.7	100.1	101.7	100.6	104.1
1970	108.3	99.3	103.7	100.4	107.8
1971	108.2	96.5	104.9	98.5	109.8
1972	113.8	95.3	104.5	97.5	116.7
1973	113.3	95.0	105.3	97.4	116.3
1974	104.9	94.4	106.1	97.2	107.9
1975	112.9	92.6	106.0	95.8	117.8
1976	126.5	94.2	107.6	97.4	129.8
1973 I	113.2	97.1	104.8	99.1	114.2
1973 II	112.2	94.0	104.7	96.8	116.0
1973 III	113.3	94.8	103.9	97.2	116.6
1973 IV	114.3	95.4	105.2	97.9	116.8
1974 I	111.9	95.8	104.9	98.2	114.0
1974 II	110.5	94.6	105.7	97.4	113.4
1974 III	99.9	95.0	105.7	97.8	102.1
1974 IV	97.4	92.7	106.0	96.1	101.3
1975 I	106.5	91.4	104.4	94.7	112.5
1975 II	110.4	91.4	104.0	94.6	116.7
1975 III	118.4	93.6	105.0	96.5	122.7
1975 IV	116.3	93.7	106.0	96.8	120.1
1976 I	121.8	94.2	106.6	97.4	125.0
1976 II	124.1	94.2	107.7	97.6	127.2
1976 III	131.7	94.1	109.3	97.9	134.5
1976 IV	128.4	94.3	109.8	98.2	130.7

TOBACCO

OUTPUT, INPUTS, AND PRODUCTIVITY RATIOS
(1967=100)

	REAL OUTPUT	LABOR INPUT	CAPITAL INPUT	TOTAL FACTOR INPUT	TOTAL FACTOR PRODUCTIVITY
1948	65.7	132.4	80.9	103.4	63.5
1949	70.6	123.8	86.1	102.5	68.9
1950	66.8	118.7	82.6	98.2	67.9
1951	80.7	120.7	99.9	108.6	74.2
1952	78.2	121.4	101.3	109.7	71.3
1953	71.9	118.0	99.9	107.4	67.0
1954	67.6	116.9	96.7	105.2	64.3
1955	71.9	118.9	102.4	109.2	65.9
1956	76.0	116.0	95.6	104.1	73.0
1957	79.3	112.2	97.1	103.3	76.8
1958	84.7	111.2	95.7	102.1	83.0
1959	89.6	111.1	100.1	104.4	85.9
1960	92.6	108.7	102.4	104.9	88.3
1961	96.5	106.4	109.7	108.4	89.0
1962	100.0	104.8	105.4	105.2	95.1
1963	100.8	102.5	103.3	103.0	97.9
1964	97.0	104.8	101.6	102.8	94.3
1965	95.9	98.3	101.9	100.5	95.5
1966	97.5	99.0	97.6	98.2	99.3
1967	100.0	100.0	100.0	100.0	100.0
1968	102.5	95.9	95.3	95.6	107.2
1969	104.4	92.7	95.6	94.5	110.4
1970	109.8	94.4	95.6	95.2	115.4
1971	111.4	87.9	98.8	94.4	118.0
1972	115.3	84.5	102.5	95.3	121.0
1973	119.1	91.9	98.2	95.7	124.5
1974	120.7	90.9	104.7	99.2	121.7
1975	122.9	89.7	101.5	96.8	127.0
1976	126.4	87.4	105.6	98.3	128.6
1973 I	117.9	88.5	96.9	94.0	125.3
1973 II	118.0	90.1	97.5	95.0	124.2
1973 III	118.1	89.5	97.7	94.9	124.4
1973 IV	122.4	96.5	98.0	97.9	125.0
1974 I	122.0	91.9	99.1	96.7	126.2
1974 II	120.6	90.1	101.3	97.3	124.0
1974 III	120.8	90.8	102.2	98.1	123.1
1974 IV	119.4	89.5	104.6	99.0	120.6
1975 I	118.7	88.9	100.2	96.2	123.4
1975 II	124.8	86.1	98.2	93.8	133.0
1975 III	122.8	88.1	98.7	94.9	129.4
1975 IV	125.3	91.8	101.4	98.0	127.8
1976 I	129.4	90.6	103.1	98.6	131.3
1976 II	124.3	87.8	105.4	98.8	125.7
1976 III	124.0	85.2	106.1	98.2	126.3
1976 IV	128.3	84.6	105.1	97.4	131.8

TEXTILES

OUTPUT, INPUTS, AND PRODUCTIVITY RATIOS
(1967=100)

	REAL OUTPUT	LABOR INPUT	CAPITAL INPUT	TOTAL FACTOR INPUT	TOTAL FACTOR PRODUCTIVITY
1948	56.1	134.4	47.2	111.6	50.2
1949	51.2	115.4	52.9	99.1	51.6
1950	53.7	127.6	62.4	110.7	48.5
1951	56.3	122.7	70.7	109.3	51.5
1952	55.4	115.6	70.6	104.0	53.3
1953	54.4	114.5	74.2	104.2	52.2
1954	51.5	102.0	76.8	95.6	53.8
1955	57.3	107.1	81.3	100.6	56.9
1956	58.3	104.4	86.9	100.1	58.3
1957	57.0	97.6	85.7	94.7	60.2
1958	56.1	90.9	87.2	90.2	62.2
1959	61.1	98.0	90.1	96.3	63.5
1960	59.4	94.1	90.5	93.2	63.7
1961	59.8	91.5	89.6	91.1	65.6
1962	63.9	93.6	89.3	92.6	68.9
1963	80.9	91.7	90.2	91.3	88.5
1964	86.1	93.0	90.6	92.5	93.2
1965	94.3	98.2	92.5	96.9	97.3
1966	103.4	102.3	97.1	101.2	102.2
1967	100.0	100.0	100.0	100.0	100.0
1968	105.1	104.8	102.4	104.2	100.9
1969	106.9	104.3	104.4	104.3	102.4
1970	111.6	99.9	104.4	100.8	110.8
1971	113.7	99.7	107.4	101.1	112.5
1972	123.4	105.1	107.6	105.6	116.9
1973	123.5	107.8	110.3	108.2	114.1
1974	116.9	99.6	113.1	102.1	114.5
1975	108.6	91.0	111.2	94.7	114.6
1976	118.7	99.4	112.3	101.8	116.6
1973 I	124.7	109.6	109.1	109.6	113.8
1973 II	124.1	107.5	109.4	107.9	115.0
1973 III	120.5	106.4	109.7	107.1	112.5
1973 IV	124.6	106.1	110.2	107.0	116.4
1974 I	124.9	105.3	110.6	106.4	117.4
1974 II	126.2	102.5	111.3	104.2	121.1
1974 III	115.3	100.1	112.4	102.5	112.5
1974 IV	101.1	89.8	113.1	94.2	107.4
1975 I	93.6	80.2	111.4	86.1	108.7
1975 II	111.7	87.7	110.9	92.1	121.2
1975 III	112.7	94.8	111.1	97.9	115.1
1975 IV	116.4	100.1	111.2	102.2	113.8
1976 I	120.4	101.0	111.2	103.0	116.9
1976 II	119.8	100.0	111.9	102.3	117.0
1976 III	118.5	98.0	112.2	100.8	117.6
1976 IV	116.2	97.7	112.1	100.5	115.7

APPAREL

OUTPUT, INPUTS, AND PRODUCTIVITY RATIOS
(1967=100)

	REAL OUTPUT	LABOR INPUT	CAPITAL INPUT	TOTAL FACTOR INPUT	TOTAL FACTOR PRODUCTIVITY
1948	58.5	86.6	70.1	85.1	68.8
1949	58.3	84.7	68.1	83.1	70.2
1950	63.3	87.4	70.4	85.8	73.8
1951	67.0	86.4	67.5	84.6	79.2
1952	68.5	88.2	67.8	86.2	79.5
1953	69.2	89.8	67.9	87.6	79.0
1954	65.0	83.8	65.6	82.1	79.2
1955	69.8	88.4	66.8	86.2	80.9
1956	71.3	88.0	59.4	85.0	83.9
1957	70.3	86.6	61.0	84.0	83.7
1958	69.0	82.7	59.9	80.3	85.9
1959	73.4	89.3	61.0	86.4	85.0
1960	75.9	88.4	61.5	85.6	88.7
1961	74.6	86.5	63.8	84.2	88.6
1962	79.2	91.5	71.9	89.4	88.5
1963	81.9	92.6	71.7	90.4	90.5
1964	85.8	92.9	80.1	91.6	93.7
1965	92.6	98.4	87.5	97.2	95.3
1966	100.7	101.5	94.0	100.7	100.0
1967	100.0	100.0	100.0	100.0	100.0
1968	105.3	100.5	112.5	101.7	103.5
1969	104.0	100.3	111.3	101.5	102.5
1970	100.9	96.2	116.2	98.3	102.7
1971	103.7	95.5	117.9	97.9	106.0
1972	116.4	98.4	126.2	101.3	114.9
1973	131.9	100.5	131.6	103.8	127.1
1974	121.1	94.3	139.1	99.0	122.3
1975	122.1	86.8	137.2	92.1	132.6
1976	133.3	92.2	141.1	97.3	136.9
1973 I	124.4	102.7	129.9	105.7	117.7
1973 II	129.4	100.8	131.0	104.1	124.3
1973 III	139.0	99.5	131.0	102.9	135.1
1973 IV	134.6	98.9	131.4	102.5	131.4
1974 I	128.0	97.5	133.0	101.4	126.3
1974 II	126.1	95.2	134.3	99.4	126.9
1974 III	116.5	95.1	137.0	99.6	116.9
1974 IV	113.7	88.9	139.0	94.2	120.6
1975 I	111.2	81.2	136.9	87.2	127.6
1975 II	117.3	83.6	136.0	89.2	131.4
1975 III	127.6	88.7	137.3	94.0	135.8
1975 IV	132.4	93.4	137.1	98.1	135.0
1976 I	134.8	95.3	137.9	99.9	135.0
1976 II	134.4	93.7	139.9	98.7	136.2
1976 III	130.3	90.5	140.7	95.9	135.9
1976 IV	133.4	89.2	140.5	94.7	140.8

LUMBER

OUTPUT, INPUTS, AND PRODUCTIVITY RATIOS
(1967=100)

	REAL OUTPUT	LABOR INPUT	CAPITAL INPUT	TOTAL FACTOR INPUT	TOTAL FACTOR PRODUCTIVITY
1948	64.1	137.8	141.0	136.9	46.8
1949	55.9	123.7	129.1	123.5	45.3
1950	59.7	133.3	119.7	128.5	46.4
1951	60.6	137.2	116.0	130.5	46.4
1952	59.8	130.4	108.9	123.7	48.3
1953	56.6	126.0	101.2	118.6	47.7
1954	54.6	116.9	96.7	110.7	49.3
1955	63.3	122.2	93.5	113.9	55.5
1956	63.0	118.6	92.2	110.9	56.8
1957	59.1	106.6	80.2	99.1	59.7
1958	54.8	101.3	76.5	94.2	58.2
1959	64.6	111.3	73.7	101.1	63.9
1960	61.3	105.2	79.9	98.3	62.3
1961	58.2	99.5	79.2	94.0	61.9
1962	58.2	100.3	82.1	95.3	61.0
1963	71.7	97.7	85.1	94.3	76.0
1964	87.8	100.4	89.7	97.5	90.1
1965	98.3	102.7	94.7	100.5	97.8
1966	96.5	103.4	98.1	102.0	94.7
1967	100.0	100.0	100.0	100.0	100.0
1968	105.0	98.7	102.5	99.7	105.2
1969	102.7	101.0	109.9	103.4	99.3
1970	107.4	95.0	113.2	100.6	106.7
1971	107.1	97.4	118.2	103.9	103.1
1972	118.6	104.5	124.9	110.8	107.0
1973	121.0	84.3	134.3	100.8	120.1
1974	118.5	102.3	145.7	116.5	101.7
1975	107.0	89.3	147.8	108.7	98.4
1976	121.4	98.7	153.6	116.8	104.0
1973 I	121.1	113.9	127.4	118.2	102.5
1973 II	121.1	113.2	128.0	117.9	102.7
1973 III	120.4	111.9	130.8	118.1	101.9
1973 IV	121.7	111.5	134.2	119.0	102.3
1974 I	123.0	111.2	136.6	119.6	102.9
1974 II	125.1	111.5	139.5	120.8	103.6
1974 III	120.6	106.4	151.6	121.6	99.2
1974 IV	105.3	96.2	146.0	113.0	93.2
1975 I	102.3	87.3	146.8	107.4	95.2
1975 II	114.4	90.0	146.5	109.1	104.9
1975 III	106.6	92.3	146.7	110.6	96.4
1975 IV	104.6	95.1	148.0	112.9	92.6
1976 I	119.6	98.9	147.9	115.4	103.6
1976 II	118.1	99.0	149.2	115.9	101.9
1976 III	123.1	100.4	151.8	117.7	104.6
1976 IV	124.9	102.7	153.6	119.8	104.3

FURNITURE

OUTPUT, INPUTS, AND PRODUCTIVITY RATIOS
(1967=100)

	REAL OUTPUT	LABOR INPUT	CAPITAL INPUT	TOTAL FACTOR INPUT	TOTAL FACTOR PRODUCTIVITY
1948	58.0	80.9	88.4	81.7	70.9
1949	55.1	72.9	85.3	74.4	74.1
1950	66.6	85.8	88.6	86.1	77.4
1951	63.4	82.7	96.7	84.4	75.2
1952	70.2	82.8	99.4	84.8	82.8
1953	68.1	84.6	99.0	86.3	79.0
1954	65.8	77.2	96.5	79.6	82.7
1955	76.0	84.4	100.0	86.2	88.1
1956	76.5	85.4	106.4	88.0	86.9
1957	73.1	83.8	80.9	83.4	87.7
1958	66.8	79.8	80.6	79.8	83.7
1959	76.2	88.0	81.6	87.1	87.5
1960	75.7	86.5	83.8	86.1	88.0
1961	72.6	82.8	80.7	82.5	88.0
1962	78.6	87.6	83.7	87.0	90.3
1963	81.7	87.5	84.3	87.1	93.9
1964	88.8	91.1	84.7	90.2	98.4
1965	99.5	97.1	91.8	96.3	103.3
1966	105.5	102.5	99.9	102.1	103.3
1967	100.0	100.0	100.0	100.0	100.0
1968	106.3	102.9	101.8	102.7	103.4
1969	115.4	104.7	108.9	105.3	109.6
1970	100.5	96.9	106.1	98.1	102.4
1971	104.7	98.7	107.0	99.8	104.9
1972	125.3	108.8	113.0	109.4	114.6
1973	132.1	115.0	119.9	115.7	114.2
1974	123.0	108.3	127.8	110.9	110.9
1975	107.6	92.5	124.2	96.6	111.4
1976	123.5	102.0	129.2	105.5	117.1
1973 I	129.6	116.9	114.1	116.9	110.8
1973 II	130.1	115.5	117.0	116.1	112.1
1973 III	131.8	115.0	117.9	115.8	113.9
1973 IV	137.0	115.3	119.8	116.2	117.9
1974 I	131.9	113.2	123.1	114.8	114.9
1974 II	134.8	111.9	126.9	114.1	118.2
1974 III	118.8	110.1	127.3	112.6	105.4
1974 IV	106.4	101.2	128.0	104.9	101.5
1975 I	99.7	87.8	121.2	92.3	108.1
1975 II	103.0	89.2	121.3	93.5	110.2
1975 III	112.5	93.9	123.3	97.9	114.9
1975 IV	115.1	99.5	124.5	102.9	111.8
1976 I	122.7	102.5	127.4	105.9	115.8
1976 II	121.9	103.3	129.0	106.8	114.1
1976 III	123.8	101.5	128.9	105.3	117.5
1976 IV	125.3	102.4	129.2	106.1	118.2

PAPER

OUTPUT, INPUTS, AND PRODUCTIVITY RATIOS
(1967=100)

	REAL OUTPUT	LABOR INPUT	CAPITAL INPUT	TOTAL FACTOR INPUT	TOTAL FACTOR PRODUCTIVITY
1948	47.0	70.3	56.2	65.7	71.5
1949	46.7	66.2	58.0	63.6	73.5
1950	60.8	72.7	59.9	68.5	88.8
1951	65.0	76.0	62.2	71.4	91.0
1952	59.9	73.9	64.1	70.7	84.6
1953	63.4	78.0	65.4	73.9	85.8
1954	65.1	77.3	67.3	74.1	87.9
1955	71.7	81.3	70.1	77.7	92.3
1956	73.8	83.4	73.3	80.2	92.1
1957	68.3	83.1	75.7	80.8	84.5
1958	68.8	81.6	76.9	80.2	85.8
1959	77.2	86.9	78.5	84.3	91.6
1960	76.0	87.8	79.9	85.3	89.0
1961	79.7	88.4	81.5	86.2	92.4
1962	83.4	90.0	83.3	87.9	94.8
1963	84.8	91.0	84.7	89.0	95.3
1964	91.2	91.9	86.5	90.2	101.0
1965	95.9	94.5	90.0	93.1	103.0
1966	102.7	99.2	95.2	97.9	104.9
1967	100.0	100.0	100.0	100.0	100.0
1968	109.9	102.2	102.4	102.3	107.5
1969	120.0	105.2	106.6	105.6	113.6
1970	109.7	102.5	108.9	104.5	105.0
1971	117.2	99.2	110.3	102.6	114.3
1972	131.7	101.5	111.1	104.4	126.1
1973	149.3	104.1	113.1	106.8	139.8
1974	139.2	102.0	117.5	106.7	130.4
1975	112.4	92.8	119.2	100.8	111.5
1976	133.8	99.2	123.0	106.4	125.7
1973 I	140.8	105.7	111.3	107.9	130.5
1973 II	143.9	102.6	111.5	105.8	136.0
1973 III	153.3	102.8	112.3	106.2	144.3
1973 IV	159.4	103.1	113.1	106.7	149.4
1974 I	149.3	104.1	113.2	107.4	139.0
1974 II	151.9	102.6	114.4	106.8	142.3
1974 III	132.7	102.3	115.9	107.0	124.0
1974 IV	122.8	97.5	117.5	104.1	118.0
1975 I	111.6	91.8	116.9	99.9	111.7
1975 II	113.7	89.3	117.3	98.3	115.6
1975 III	109.9	92.8	118.2	101.0	108.7
1975 IV	114.5	96.0	119.2	103.5	110.6
1976 I	131.7	98.5	119.5	105.4	124.9
1976 II	136.7	99.5	120.8	106.5	128.4
1976 III	133.9	99.0	122.3	106.6	125.6
1976 IV	133.2	99.4	123.4	107.2	124.3

PRINTING AND PUBLISHING

OUTPUT, INPUTS, AND PRODUCTIVITY RATIOS
(1967=100)

	REAL OUTPUT	LABOR INPUT	CAPITAL INPUT	TOTAL FACTOR INPUT	TOTAL FACTOR PRODUCTIVITY
1948	50.6	76.8	73.4	76.0	66.5
1949	53.0	75.6	73.5	75.0	70.7
1950	53.5	75.7	73.9	75.2	71.1
1951	54.6	77.0	74.2	76.3	71.6
1952	55.7	77.5	73.0	76.5	72.8
1953	58.0	79.6	71.6	78.0	74.3
1954	61.0	80.1	70.7	78.2	78.0
1955	65.0	82.5	70.9	80.2	81.0
1956	67.5	85.0	70.2	82.2	82.1
1957	68.4	85.3	69.5	82.4	83.0
1958	66.7	84.3	69.8	81.5	81.8
1959	71.3	87.1	69.7	83.8	85.1
1960	73.1	89.3	73.8	86.4	84.6
1961	74.0	89.1	76.1	86.7	85.4
1962	77.0	89.6	79.4	87.6	87.9
1963	83.6	90.3	82.7	88.9	94.1
1964	91.5	91.7	85.6	90.6	101.1
1965	94.4	95.2	88.5	93.9	100.5
1966	99.0	97.9	95.3	97.4	101.6
1967	100.0	100.0	100.0	100.0	100.0
1968	102.7	101.3	104.0	101.8	100.9
1969	107.9	104.1	112.6	105.7	102.2
1970	101.7	103.5	115.7	105.9	96.1
1971	102.7	100.0	118.8	103.7	99.1
1972	108.0	101.9	120.9	105.6	102.3
1973	115.1	105.4	126.1	109.4	105.2
1974	108.2	104.9	130.5	109.9	98.5
1975	102.5	101.6	131.8	107.6	95.3
1976	111.3	102.7	135.7	109.2	101.9
1973 I	111.4	108.0	123.8	111.5	99.9
1973 II	112.6	105.4	124.7	109.5	102.8
1973 III	118.4	105.9	124.9	110.0	107.7
1973 IV	117.9	105.7	126.0	110.0	107.1
1974 I	112.5	105.2	125.8	109.6	102.6
1974 II	116.5	105.7	119.6	108.7	107.1
1974 III	104.5	106.4	129.0	111.2	94.0
1974 IV	99.5	105.1	130.4	110.5	90.1
1975 I	101.4	102.9	129.0	108.4	93.6
1975 II	101.0	100.5	128.7	106.4	94.9
1975 III	104.3	99.9	129.7	106.1	98.3
1975 IV	103.3	100.8	131.7	107.3	96.3
1976 I	110.8	101.3	133.0	107.9	102.7
1976 II	111.4	101.7	134.6	108.6	102.7
1976 III	111.7	102.3	135.0	109.1	102.4
1976 IV	111.2	103.1	135.6	109.9	101.2

CHEMICALS

OUTPUT, INPUTS, AND PRODUCTIVITY RATIOS
(1967=100)

	REAL OUTPUT	LABOR INPUT	CAPITAL INPUT	TOTAL FACTOR INPUT	TOTAL FACTOR PRODUCTIVITY
1948	30.6	66.6	42.4	55.6	54.9
1949	30.0	62.3	45.4	54.7	54.8
1950	35.9	64.7	48.5	57.4	62.5
1951	38.3	71.2	53.1	63.1	60.8
1952	38.7	72.3	57.5	65.7	58.9
1953	41.5	76.1	60.8	69.2	60.0
1954	43.6	74.7	63.7	69.8	62.6
1955	50.3	76.9	66.7	72.4	69.6
1956	52.7	79.3	70.4	75.3	69.9
1957	55.0	80.5	73.6	77.4	71.0
1958	54.1	78.7	76.3	77.7	69.6
1959	62.2	81.7	78.8	80.5	77.3
1960	62.6	83.7	79.6	82.0	76.4
1961	65.0	83.6	81.2	82.6	78.7
1962	69.9	85.6	82.6	84.3	82.9
1963	77.9	87.0	83.8	85.7	90.9
1964	84.4	88.1	86.0	87.2	96.7
1965	92.3	91.5	90.2	90.9	101.6
1966	98.7	96.5	95.6	96.1	102.6
1967	100.0	100.0	100.0	100.0	100.0
1968	113.6	103.7	103.6	103.6	109.6
1969	119.7	106.4	107.6	106.9	112.0
1970	120.8	105.4	111.4	107.8	112.1
1971	125.0	101.4	113.2	106.0	117.9
1972	135.9	101.1	114.0	106.2	128.0
1973	146.6	104.8	115.8	109.1	134.3
1974	136.4	105.7	120.7	111.6	122.2
1975	132.8	100.1	121.5	108.4	122.4
1976	146.3	103.6	124.5	111.8	130.9
1973 I	145.1	106.2	114.0	110.0	132.0
1973 II	147.2	103.6	114.4	108.5	135.6
1973 III	145.9	103.7	115.1	108.8	134.1
1973 IV	148.0	104.2	115.8	109.4	135.3
1974 I	141.3	105.9	115.9	110.5	127.8
1974 II	144.3	106.4	116.9	111.2	129.8
1974 III	133.0	105.8	118.9	111.6	119.2
1974 IV	126.8	104.0	120.7	111.2	114.0
1975 I	125.4	101.1	119.8	109.1	115.0
1975 II	130.5	98.9	120.6	108.1	120.8
1975 III	135.0	99.7	121.1	108.7	124.2
1975 IV	140.1	101.8	121.5	110.2	127.2
1976 I	145.3	103.1	122.2	111.2	130.6
1976 II	145.1	103.6	122.8	111.8	129.7
1976 III	146.0	103.7	124.3	112.5	129.8
1976 IV	148.8	104.1	125.2	113.0	131.7

PETROLEUM

OUTPUT, INPUTS, AND PRODUCTIVITY RATIOS
(1967=100)

	REAL OUTPUT	LABOR INPUT	CAPITAL INPUT	TOTAL FACTOR INPUT	TOTAL FACTOR PRODUCTIVITY
1948	50.2	120.0	60.3	81.3	61.8
1949	50.4	116.0	63.3	81.9	61.5
1950	57.7	115.0	63.7	81.8	70.5
1951	58.3	121.4	66.6	86.0	67.8
1952	59.0	121.5	70.1	88.4	66.7
1953	62.5	125.4	74.4	92.6	67.5
1954	60.9	124.5	77.1	94.1	64.7
1955	68.8	124.2	79.7	95.8	71.9
1956	70.6	123.9	82.8	97.7	72.3
1957	69.8	122.0	88.8	101.1	69.0
1958	69.3	118.1	87.4	98.8	70.1
1959	77.1	114.8	87.1	97.5	79.0
1960	78.8	113.1	88.0	97.4	80.9
1961	82.1	107.8	89.9	96.6	84.9
1962	88.0	104.7	91.6	96.5	91.2
1963	91.1	100.5	92.2	95.3	95.6
1964	93.1	97.6	92.5	94.4	98.5
1965	97.6	98.3	94.0	95.6	102.0
1966	100.0	99.8	95.7	97.3	102.8
1967	100.0	100.0	100.0	100.0	100.0
1968	107.9	101.1	104.0	102.9	104.9
1969	109.4	98.8	107.2	104.0	105.1
1970	116.0	104.3	110.9	108.3	107.1
1971	119.1	105.2	114.0	110.7	107.5
1972	122.3	104.6	114.8	111.1	110.1
1973	128.9	105.2	115.8	111.9	115.2
1974	125.2	107.6	121.5	116.5	107.5
1975	122.3	105.3	123.9	117.3	104.2
1976	132.1	109.7	127.0	120.9	109.3
1973 I	127.1	105.1	114.9	112.8	112.6
1973 II	130.4	102.3	115.4	112.2	116.2
1973 III	128.9	106.5	115.4	113.6	113.4
1973 IV	129.4	106.4	115.8	113.9	113.6
1974 I	120.9	106.6	116.3	114.2	105.9
1974 II	129.5	108.9	118.2	116.3	111.3
1974 III	125.3	107.4	120.0	117.1	107.0
1974 IV	125.0	107.3	121.5	118.0	106.0
1975 I	123.7	103.2	121.2	116.5	106.2
1975 II	124.1	104.0	121.9	117.2	105.9
1975 III	122.7	105.5	123.1	118.5	103.5
1975 IV	118.7	107.9	123.8	119.8	99.1
1976 I	128.1	110.4	124.6	121.2	105.7
1976 II	132.6	109.8	125.3	121.5	109.2
1976 III	133.4	109.0	126.7	122.1	109.3
1976 IV	134.4	109.6	127.4	122.8	109.4

RUBBER

OUTPUT, INPUTS, AND PRODUCTIVITY RATIOS
(1967=100)

	REAL OUTPUT	LABOR INPUT	CAPITAL INPUT	TOTAL FACTOR INPUT	TOTAL FACTOR PRODUCTIVITY
1948	37.8	58.1	48.2	55.7	67.8
1949	34.4	51.9	49.9	51.4	67.0
1950	40.2	60.3	46.2	56.9	70.7
1951	50.2	64.1	54.4	61.7	81.4
1952	49.9	64.6	58.6	63.1	79.1
1953	50.1	68.1	62.1	66.6	75.2
1954	44.9	61.4	63.5	61.9	72.5
1955	50.1	71.0	64.9	69.5	72.0
1956	48.7	69.8	68.5	69.5	70.1
1957	48.4	70.9	70.5	70.8	68.4
1958	46.7	63.6	73.0	65.8	71.0
1959	59.0	72.5	75.6	73.3	80.6
1960	58.7	71.5	76.3	72.7	80.8
1961	61.5	71.3	77.9	72.9	84.3
1962	70.6	78.5	80.4	79.0	89.4
1963	77.2	80.1	81.5	80.4	96.0
1964	83.5	84.5	85.3	84.7	98.5
1965	90.7	92.5	89.5	91.8	98.8
1966	98.5	100.0	94.5	98.7	99.7
1967	100.0	100.0	100.0	100.0	100.0
1968	113.4	109.3	107.2	108.8	104.2
1969	125.9	115.0	114.9	115.0	109.5
1970	112.7	110.1	120.2	112.2	100.5
1971	121.1	110.1	123.4	112.8	107.3
1972	136.0	120.3	130.5	122.4	111.1
1973	154.0	131.0	140.2	132.9	115.9
1974	138.2	128.0	145.2	131.5	105.1
1975	120.3	110.2	141.2	116.6	103.2
1976	135.7	117.4	141.7	122.4	110.8
1973 I	148.0	133.0	133.3	133.5	110.9
1973 II	148.2	129.5	134.9	131.1	113.0
1973 III	157.0	129.2	137.9	131.5	119.5
1973 IV	162.8	130.5	140.1	132.9	122.5
1974 I	149.5	130.5	141.6	133.3	112.2
1974 II	153.1	127.7	142.6	131.2	116.7
1974 III	131.6	129.5	144.3	133.1	98.9
1974 IV	118.7	122.8	145.1	127.9	92.8
1975 I	107.6	108.2	142.8	115.7	93.0
1975 II	116.8	106.6	142.3	114.3	102.2
1975 III	128.6	111.5	140.7	117.9	109.1
1975 IV	128.3	114.6	141.1	120.5	106.5
1976 I	134.9	118.4	140.6	123.4	109.3
1976 II	129.7	113.3	139.7	119.1	108.9
1976 III	133.5	112.7	139.6	118.7	112.5
1976 IV	144.6	125.1	140.6	128.8	112.3

LEATHER

OUTPUT, INPUTS, AND PRODUCTIVITY RATIOS
(1967=100)

	REAL OUTPUT	LABOR INPUT	CAPITAL INPUT	TOTAL FACTOR INPUT	TOTAL FACTOR PRODUCTIVITY
1948	97.9	115.9	99.3	114.1	85.8
1949	87.1	108.1	98.0	107.2	81.2
1950	86.7	111.9	125.5	114.4	75.7
1951	92.9	105.2	107.4	106.1	87.6
1952	81.7	110.0	124.5	112.7	72.5
1953	86.7	109.2	123.6	111.9	77.5
1954	79.6	103.1	123.9	106.7	74.6
1955	83.7	109.2	130.6	112.8	74.2
1956	84.2	107.5	92.8	106.0	79.4
1957	82.5	104.6	94.0	103.6	79.6
1958	77.9	99.1	92.3	98.6	79.0
1959	93.3	106.7	88.9	104.7	89.2
1960	87.1	101.4	89.4	100.0	87.1
1961	85.8	101.0	86.5	99.3	86.4
1962	94.2	101.6	86.2	99.9	94.3
1963	95.8	99.3	96.3	99.0	96.8
1964	98.3	98.0	90.1	97.1	101.3
1965	103.3	100.3	93.9	99.5	103.8
1966	108.7	104.6	101.9	104.3	104.3
1967	100.0	100.0	100.0	100.0	100.0
1968	104.2	101.6	108.1	102.3	101.8
1969	100.4	95.0	114.9	97.3	103.2
1970	93.7	89.8	115.2	92.8	101.1
1971	89.6	85.6	115.7	89.2	100.4
1972	89.6	86.2	115.8	89.7	99.8
1973	97.5	82.8	116.8	86.9	112.1
1974	90.0	77.2	122.4	82.9	108.6
1975	82.9	71.7	115.7	77.3	107.3
1976	93.7	75.7	115.5	80.7	116.2
1973 I	94.4	85.1	117.3	89.1	105.9
1973 II	95.2	83.3	117.8	87.6	108.7
1973 III	99.2	81.9	117.3	86.3	114.9
1973 IV	101.2	80.8	116.7	85.3	118.7
1974 I	96.6	79.9	117.0	84.5	114.3
1974 II	97.1	79.1	121.9	84.6	114.8
1974 III	86.4	76.3	123.0	82.3	105.0
1974 IV	79.9	72.6	122.3	79.0	101.1
1975 I	76.4	66.7	116.3	73.1	104.6
1975 II	79.6	69.3	116.4	75.3	105.8
1975 III	86.5	73.3	116.4	78.8	109.7
1975 IV	89.1	77.6	115.6	82.4	108.1
1976 I	97.1	79.4	114.4	83.8	115.9
1976 II	100.4	78.1	114.1	82.7	121.5
1976 III	90.0	73.6	113.9	78.7	114.4
1976 IV	86.3	71.6	115.0	77.2	111.8

STONE, CLAY AND GLASS

OUTPUT, INPUTS, AND PRODUCTIVITY RATIOS
(1967=100)

	REAL OUTPUT	LABOR INPUT	CAPITAL INPUT	TOTAL FACTOR INPUT	TOTAL FACTOR PRODUCTIVITY
1948	57.5	87.5	48.7	75.9	75.8
1949	53.7	80.3	50.0	71.2	75.4
1950	64.3	87.6	52.4	77.1	83.4
1951	69.0	94.2	56.3	82.9	83.3
1952	66.3	89.4	58.2	80.1	82.8
1953	70.1	91.4	60.0	82.0	85.5
1954	68.3	86.8	61.5	79.2	86.2
1955	78.8	93.9	65.5	85.4	92.2
1956	77.6	95.9	70.9	88.5	87.7
1957	75.3	93.1	74.6	87.6	86.0
1958	73.4	87.3	76.5	84.1	87.3
1959	83.2	96.6	81.9	92.2	90.1
1960	81.7	95.3	84.3	92.1	88.8
1961	81.6	92.1	85.6	90.2	90.5
1962	85.9	93.6	86.3	91.4	93.9
1963	93.1	95.2	88.8	93.3	99.8
1964	99.5	98.3	91.1	96.2	103.5
1965	103.1	100.7	92.8	98.3	104.8
1966	103.9	103.2	97.5	101.5	102.4
1967	100.0	100.0	100.0	100.0	100.0
1968	103.3	101.8	100.2	101.3	102.0
1969	109.6	105.1	103.4	104.6	104.8
1970	103.9	101.1	106.2	102.3	101.5
1971	105.8	101.2	107.0	102.6	103.1
1972	117.1	105.3	110.1	106.5	110.0
1973	125.7	112.0	113.6	112.4	111.9
1974	112.9	109.5	117.8	111.5	101.3
1975	102.8	96.3	117.4	101.5	101.3
1976	113.8	99.3	120.1	104.4	108.9
1973 I	121.0	111.0	109.7	110.9	109.1
1973 II	122.3	111.8	110.2	111.6	109.6
1973 III	127.4	112.7	111.8	112.7	113.0
1973 IV	132.2	112.6	113.6	113.1	117.0
1974 I	122.7	111.4	114.1	112.3	109.3
1974 II	122.6	111.4	115.5	112.6	108.9
1974 III	106.3	110.2	117.1	112.1	94.8
1974 IV	100.0	104.9	117.9	108.4	92.3
1975 I	98.2	95.9	117.1	101.4	96.8
1975 II	100.6	94.9	117.1	100.7	99.9
1975 III	105.5	95.4	117.1	101.0	104.4
1975 IV	107.2	96.9	117.5	102.2	104.8
1976 I	109.8	97.6	117.3	102.7	106.9
1976 II	112.1	99.5	118.0	104.3	107.5
1976 III	115.2	99.0	119.1	104.3	110.5
1976 IV	117.7	100.1	120.1	105.3	111.7

PRIMARY METALS

OUTPUT, INPUTS, AND PRODUCTIVITY RATIOS
(1967=100)

	REAL OUTPUT	LABOR INPUT	CAPITAL INPUT	TOTAL FACTOR INPUT	TOTAL FACTOR PRODUCTIVITY
1948	72.1	96.4	50.2	82.7	87.1
1949	64.4	81.3	51.4	72.5	88.9
1950	76.1	94.5	53.5	82.4	92.3
1951	91.7	104.8	56.8	90.6	101.3
1952	82.5	96.0	61.3	85.8	96.2
1953	94.4	103.9	65.2	92.5	102.0
1954	73.3	87.3	66.7	81.3	90.2
1955	89.6	100.3	68.9	91.1	98.4
1956	88.6	102.2	73.8	93.9	94.4
1957	89.3	99.0	77.8	92.9	96.2
1958	67.9	81.5	81.3	81.6	83.2
1959	75.2	88.5	81.3	86.5	86.9
1960	74.4	89.0	83.7	87.6	84.9
1961	70.3	83.7	85.2	84.1	83.6
1962	75.2	86.4	85.5	86.2	87.3
1963	80.3	88.5	86.6	88.0	91.3
1964	90.6	94.7	88.4	93.0	97.4
1965	98.5	100.7	91.1	98.1	100.4
1966	105.1	104.2	95.5	101.8	103.2
1967	100.0	100.0	100.0	100.0	100.0
1968	99.5	100.8	103.2	101.5	98.0
1969	98.6	104.6	105.6	104.9	94.0
1970	90.0	98.4	108.5	100.8	89.3
1971	85.0	91.9	108.9	95.8	88.7
1972	92.3	95.0	109.4	98.4	93.8
1973	106.2	104.0	109.0	105.2	100.9
1974	105.7	103.4	111.2	105.2	100.4
1975	84.8	87.6	114.2	93.8	90.4
1976	85.8	89.4	116.5	95.7	89.6
1973 I	97.0	104.6	108.7	106.0	91.4
1973 II	95.3	101.8	108.7	103.8	91.8
1973 III	115.3	102.9	109.0	104.8	110.0
1973 IV	117.1	105.0	109.0	106.4	110.0
1974 I	104.7	104.0	108.0	105.4	99.4
1974 II	104.6	103.4	108.2	105.0	99.6
1974 III	108.4	103.6	109.4	105.4	102.8
1974 IV	105.0	101.1	111.1	103.9	101.1
1975 I	94.1	94.3	111.8	98.8	95.3
1975 II	88.3	86.4	113.2	93.0	95.0
1975 III	80.4	84.8	113.5	91.9	87.5
1975 IV	76.4	85.3	114.2	92.4	82.6
1976 I	81.8	87.5	114.2	94.1	87.0
1976 II	86.4	90.4	115.2	96.6	89.4
1976 III	91.5	91.4	116.1	97.5	93.8
1976 IV	83.7	88.3	117.1	95.4	87.7

FABRICATED METALS

OUTPUT, INPUTS, AND PRODUCTIVITY RATIOS
(1967=100)

	REAL OUTPUT	LABOR INPUT	CAPITAL INPUT	TOTAL FACTOR INPUT	TOTAL FACTOR PRODUCTIVITY
1948	47.7	71.7	38.6	65.0	73.3
1949	43.1	63.3	39.2	58.5	73.8
1950	51.9	73.0	42.8	66.9	77.5
1951	54.9	80.3	48.7	73.9	74.3
1952	57.2	78.7	51.6	73.2	78.1
1953	62.8	85.4	57.8	79.9	78.7
1954	59.7	77.7	56.5	73.5	81.2
1955	63.7	82.9	63.1	79.0	80.6
1956	64.5	83.5	66.6	80.2	80.4
1957	65.8	84.9	73.3	82.7	79.5
1958	61.3	76.6	72.1	75.8	80.9
1959	68.3	82.0	75.1	80.7	84.7
1960	68.6	82.4	76.1	81.2	84.5
1961	67.6	78.5	77.0	78.3	86.4
1962	73.6	82.3	79.1	81.7	90.0
1963	76.1	84.9	82.2	84.4	90.1
1964	81.8	88.0	86.0	87.6	93.4
1965	90.8	94.6	91.8	94.1	96.5
1966	98.6	100.8	96.1	99.9	98.7
1967	100.0	100.0	100.0	100.0	100.0
1968	105.4	102.8	105.1	103.2	102.1
1969	110.0	106.2	108.8	106.7	103.1
1970	99.9	99.8	112.7	102.1	97.9
1971	98.2	95.7	114.2	99.1	99.1
1972	109.8	101.5	116.5	104.2	105.4
1973	121.0	110.9	123.5	113.2	106.9
1974	108.8	108.9	128.0	112.4	96.8
1975	98.9	95.4	127.5	101.2	97.8
1976	110.3	100.4	131.6	106.1	104.0
1973 I	115.7	111.5	118.2	113.1	102.3
1973 II	117.0	110.5	118.8	112.3	104.2
1973 III	123.8	110.0	121.0	112.3	110.2
1973 IV	127.6	111.4	123.4	113.9	112.0
1974 I	115.8	110.7	124.1	113.4	102.1
1974 II	117.9	109.5	125.8	112.8	104.5
1974 III	103.5	109.8	126.2	113.1	91.5
1974 IV	97.9	105.0	128.0	109.5	89.4
1975 I	95.1	96.5	128.2	102.5	92.8
1975 II	97.3	93.9	127.6	100.2	97.1
1975 III	101.9	93.7	127.7	100.2	101.7
1975 IV	101.4	96.7	127.4	102.6	98.8
1976 I	106.7	99.3	127.4	104.7	102.0
1976 II	109.3	100.0	127.3	105.2	103.9
1976 III	112.4	101.0	129.2	106.4	105.6
1976 IV	112.8	100.4	130.7	106.2	106.3

MACHINERY EXCEPT ELECTRICAL

OUTPUT, INPUTS, AND PRODUCTIVITY RATIOS
(1967=100)

	REAL OUTPUT	LABOR INPUT	CAPITAL INPUT	TOTAL FACTOR INPUT	TOTAL FACTOR PRODUCTIVITY
1948	50.7	68.9	46.1	63.7	79.7
1949	45.2	57.3	44.2	54.3	83.1
1950	47.8	61.5	46.3	58.1	82.2
1951	62.1	76.3	52.8	70.9	87.5
1952	68.2	78.0	55.6	72.9	93.6
1953	66.6	78.7	57.9	73.9	90.1
1954	59.6	69.4	59.1	67.1	88.9
1955	60.9	72.9	61.6	70.3	86.7
1956	67.4	79.5	66.6	76.6	88.0
1957	63.6	78.2	69.9	76.3	83.3
1958	53.7	65.4	68.3	66.1	81.3
1959	62.1	72.7	69.2	71.9	86.4
1960	62.6	73.4	70.0	72.7	86.1
1961	62.1	70.3	71.0	70.5	88.2
1962	69.5	74.7	74.6	74.7	93.0
1963	72.2	77.1	76.6	77.0	93.8
1964	80.8	81.8	80.8	81.6	99.1
1965	88.8	89.4	86.1	88.7	100.1
1966	98.9	99.7	94.4	98.5	100.5
1967	100.0	100.0	100.0	100.0	100.0
1968	99.9	98.2	104.3	99.6	100.3
1969	104.5	102.6	111.5	104.7	99.8
1970	102.6	97.9	116.1	102.0	100.7
1971	96.7	88.3	116.8	94.6	102.2
1972	108.1	94.6	120.4	100.4	107.8
1973	122.3	106.8	130.2	112.0	109.2
1974	118.1	111.8	137.6	117.6	100.4
1975	113.7	101.8	137.3	109.7	103.7
1976	119.5	102.3	142.3	111.2	107.5
1973 I	114.6	106.8	122.1	114.3	100.2
1973 II	114.5	105.0	124.4	114.0	100.4
1973 III	129.6	106.0	127.2	114.3	113.4
1973 IV	130.8	109.7	130.1	116.0	112.7
1974 I	117.9	111.8	131.3	115.7	101.9
1974 II	121.2	110.6	133.3	115.3	105.1
1974 III	117.1	112.2	135.4	115.9	101.0
1974 IV	116.3	113.2	137.5	112.7	103.2
1975 I	114.5	108.1	137.6	106.0	108.0
1975 II	114.3	101.2	138.0	104.0	109.9
1975 III	114.2	98.7	138.2	104.0	109.8
1975 IV	112.0	99.7	137.2	106.1	105.6
1976 I	117.0	100.7	137.0	108.1	108.3
1976 II	118.5	101.3	137.4	108.7	109.0
1976 III	120.6	103.5	138.7	109.8	109.9
1976 IV	122.0	103.9	140.2	109.6	111.3

ELECTRICAL MACHINERY

OUTPUT, INPUTS, AND PRODUCTIVITY RATIOS
(1967=100)

	REAL OUTPUT	LABOR INPUT	CAPITAL INPUT	TOTAL FACTOR INPUT	TOTAL FACTOR PRODUCTIVITY
1948	23.1	51.0	39.9	48.8	47.4
1949	21.3	43.9	38.8	42.9	49.5
1950	25.8	52.1	39.8	49.7	51.9
1951	30.3	58.4	44.6	55.7	54.4
1952	36.7	61.8	49.0	59.3	62.0
1953	38.3	68.7	50.1	65.1	58.8
1954	34.1	60.3	47.5	57.8	59.0
1955	37.0	64.0	48.9	61.0	60.7
1956	40.2	68.5	53.4	65.5	61.3
1957	41.5	68.6	51.2	65.2	63.7
1958	39.0	62.9	51.0	60.6	64.4
1959	46.6	72.2	54.8	68.8	67.8
1960	49.3	74.8	58.4	71.6	68.8
1961	52.1	75.6	62.1	73.0	71.4
1962	59.1	80.8	67.4	78.2	75.6
1963	65.2	79.6	69.8	77.7	83.9
1964	69.4	79.4	73.2	78.2	88.7
1965	82.4	86.2	80.0	85.0	96.9
1966	96.3	99.2	91.5	97.7	98.5
1967	100.0	100.0	100.0	100.0	100.0
1968	105.6	101.2	105.8	102.1	103.4
1969	113.3	103.6	113.0	105.4	107.5
1970	106.9	97.5	116.6	101.2	105.7
1971	107.6	90.3	116.5	95.3	112.9
1972	121.6	95.0	120.3	99.9	121.7
1973	136.2	104.4	131.2	109.5	124.3
1974	131.0	103.0	136.2	109.4	119.8
1975	116.1	89.1	132.0	97.3	119.3
1976	132.6	93.7	135.2	101.7	130.4
1973 I	128.6	104.7	123.0	108.9	118.1
1973 II	129.3	102.7	124.8	107.7	120.1
1973 III	140.9	103.3	127.9	108.7	129.6
1973 IV	145.8	105.7	131.1	111.2	131.1
1974 I	136.6	105.5	132.7	111.5	122.6
1974 II	138.0	104.2	134.0	110.6	124.7
1974 III	127.1	102.4	135.4	109.5	116.1
1974 IV	122.4	98.5	136.1	106.4	115.1
1975 I	114.7	91.1	134.4	100.0	114.6
1975 II	117.9	87.5	133.0	96.9	121.8
1975 III	116.3	87.8	132.5	97.0	119.9
1975 IV	115.4	89.6	131.9	98.3	117.4
1976 I	127.0	92.3	131.8	100.5	126.4
1976 II	132.3	93.2	133.1	101.5	130.3
1976 III	134.4	93.5	134.1	101.9	131.9
1976 IV	136.6	95.2	135.1	103.5	132.0

TRANSPORTATION EQUIPMENT

OUTPUT, INPUTS, AND PRODUCTIVITY RATIOS
(1967=100)

	REAL OUTPUT	LABOR INPUT	CAPITAL INPUT	TOTAL FACTOR INPUT	TOTAL FACTOR PRODUCTIVITY
1948	31.0	56.3	42.5	52.8	58.8
1949	31.5	54.1	40.3	50.5	62.3
1950	41.4	58.9	42.3	54.6	75.7
1951	45.9	73.7	51.6	68.0	67.5
1952	53.3	91.6	54.5	82.0	65.0
1953	65.0	107.2	58.3	94.5	68.8
1954	59.5	90.6	60.4	82.8	71.9
1955	69.9	95.7	63.6	87.5	80.0
1956	60.6	93.8	68.6	87.3	69.4
1957	65.0	95.3	70.9	89.0	73.0
1958	53.7	81.9	68.5	78.5	68.3
1959	59.6	80.1	69.4	77.4	76.9
1960	61.2	78.4	69.0	76.0	80.6
1961	58.0	73.5	69.2	72.5	80.0
1962	68.7	80.9	71.8	78.6	87.4
1963	77.1	83.7	74.9	81.5	94.6
1964	80.9	82.5	78.4	81.4	99.3
1965	91.6	89.5	82.9	87.8	104.3
1966	99.5	98.4	91.3	96.6	102.9
1967	100.0	100.0	100.0	100.0	100.0
1968	112.8	106.8	106.3	106.7	105.7
1969	108.3	105.0	111.9	106.7	101.5
1970	88.4	88.3	110.0	93.7	94.3
1971	97.9	84.0	108.2	89.9	108.9
1972	105.4	87.3	112.8	93.5	112.7
1973	112.7	94.1	117.8	100.0	112.7
1974	96.3	86.1	120.9	94.7	101.8
1975	91.9	79.1	118.4	88.8	103.6
1976	114.7	84.4	120.0	93.1	123.2
1973 I	114.5	96.8	114.1	101.9	112.3
1973 II	114.9	94.3	115.0	100.3	114.6
1973 III	110.1	91.7	116.7	98.7	111.6
1973 IV	111.2	92.1	117.7	99.2	112.1
1974 I	100.0	85.5	118.5	94.4	106.0
1974 II	103.6	85.8	119.1	94.8	109.3
1974 III	95.2	86.8	120.3	95.8	99.4
1974 IV	86.4	84.6	120.8	94.3	91.6
1975 I	76.8	76.9	118.9	88.0	87.4
1975 II	80.8	78.9	119.5	89.6	90.2
1975 III	104.8	79.7	118.9	90.1	116.3
1975 IV	105.3	79.9	118.3	90.0	116.9
1976 I	110.6	84.3	117.9	93.3	118.6
1976 II	116.6	84.6	118.3	93.7	124.4
1976 III	115.4	84.1	117.4	93.0	124.0
1976 IV	116.4	83.8	117.8	93.0	125.2

INSTRUMENTS

OUTPUT, INPUTS, AND PRODUCTIVITY RATIOS
(1967=100)

	REAL OUTPUT	LABOR INPUT	CAPITAL INPUT	TOTAL FACTOR INPUT	TOTAL FACTOR PRODUCTIVITY
1948	31.2	58.0	33.0	52.0	59.9
1949	30.3	52.6	42.2	49.9	60.7
1950	35.8	56.7	45.2	53.8	66.5
1951	43.1	67.7	51.4	63.7	67.7
1952	48.9	71.1	53.3	66.7	73.3
1953	53.0	75.5	54.8	70.5	75.2
1954	52.5	69.9	55.2	66.2	79.3
1955	55.5	71.7	58.6	68.3	81.3
1956	58.4	75.1	64.2	72.3	80.9
1957	56.0	75.2	66.3	72.8	77.0
1958	55.0	70.3	67.2	69.3	79.4
1959	62.7	76.9	70.4	75.1	83.5
1960	64.2	78.4	71.6	76.5	84.0
1961	62.7	77.3	74.6	76.5	81.9
1962	69.3	79.7	79.0	79.5	87.2
1963	73.8	80.9	80.5	80.8	91.3
1964	75.0	82.2	78.9	81.3	92.3
1965	86.2	87.1	83.7	86.2	100.0
1966	99.1	97.1	92.8	95.8	103.5
1967	100.0	100.0	100.0	100.0	100.0
1968	107.5	101.0	108.5	103.1	104.2
1969	120.4	104.7	110.4	106.3	113.3
1970	107.3	100.2	113.9	104.1	103.1
1971	105.5	94.4	111.7	99.3	106.2
1972	116.4	100.1	117.4	104.9	110.9
1973	128.8	109.6	131.4	115.7	111.3
1974	121.3	112.5	141.3	120.5	100.7
1975	124.5	104.6	139.9	114.4	108.8
1976	134.2	111.0	145.0	120.4	111.5
1973 I	122.5	109.2	123.5	114.0	107.4
1973 II	123.3	107.2	125.8	113.2	108.9
1973 III	132.3	108.5	128.4	114.9	115.1
1973 IV	137.1	111.7	131.3	118.0	116.2
1974 I	129.1	113.2	134.5	120.0	107.6
1974 II	132.1	112.6	136.5	120.1	110.0
1974 III	114.3	112.7	139.6	121.0	94.5
1974 IV	109.6	110.7	141.5	120.1	91.2
1975 I	117.0	106.2	140.6	116.5	100.4
1975 II	114.3	102.8	139.6	113.8	100.4
1975 III	133.1	103.1	138.2	113.6	117.1
1975 IV	133.8	105.7	140.2	116.1	115.3
1976 I	130.2	108.8	139.7	118.2	110.1
1976 II	133.7	110.9	142.7	120.6	110.9
1976 III	135.4	110.9	143.6	120.9	112.1
1976 IV	137.5	111.9	144.9	121.9	112.7

MISCELLANEOUS MANUFACTURES

OUTPUT, INPUTS, AND PRODUCTIVITY RATIOS
(1967=100)

	REAL OUTPUT	LABOR INPUT	CAPITAL INPUT	TOTAL FACTOR INPUT	TOTAL FACTOR PRODUCTIVITY
1948	59.8	103.3	83.8	100.0	59.8
1949	53.9	92.7	73.7	89.3	60.4
1950	61.1	98.1	69.7	92.7	65.9
1951	64.1	98.5	70.7	93.2	68.8
1952	65.6	95.6	70.8	91.0	72.2
1953	68.2	101.3	62.4	93.5	72.9
1954	65.4	92.7	68.1	88.1	74.2
1955	72.5	95.2	61.3	88.5	81.9
1956	72.8	96.0	64.3	89.8	81.0
1957	71.8	92.1	62.4	86.3	83.1
1958	70.5	88.2	60.6	82.8	85.1
1959	79.1	92.9	61.1	86.7	91.3
1960	77.9	92.4	63.1	86.7	89.8
1961	79.4	90.0	63.3	84.8	93.6
1962	83.0	92.4	66.5	87.3	95.0
1963	84.5	90.7	71.3	86.9	97.2
1964	87.3	92.0	74.8	88.6	98.5
1965	92.4	98.7	78.1	94.6	97.6
1966	99.5	103.9	88.8	100.9	98.6
1967	100.0	100.0	100.0	100.0	100.0
1968	106.1	100.1	108.0	101.6	104.4
1969	110.9	101.0	110.5	102.8	107.9
1970	107.1	97.9	115.9	101.3	105.7
1971	112.2	95.1	119.2	99.6	112.6
1972	125.7	100.7	117.1	103.8	121.1
1973	128.8	103.9	119.5	106.9	120.4
1974	121.6	101.8	124.5	106.1	114.6
1975	118.8	93.8	119.4	98.6	120.5
1976	129.3	97.9	122.0	102.4	126.2
1973 I	128.9	108.4	113.9	110.1	117.1
1973 II	129.4	104.6	113.4	106.9	121.0
1973 III	127.7	103.5	116.6	106.6	119.8
1973 IV	129.0	104.8	119.4	108.2	119.3
1974 I	123.4	105.6	119.7	108.8	113.3
1974 II	128.0	105.1	122.0	108.9	117.6
1974 III	121.8	103.9	124.4	108.3	112.4
1974 IV	113.3	98.4	124.8	103.9	109.0
1975 I	111.6	92.5	120.0	98.2	113.7
1975 II	116.0	92.0	121.1	97.9	118.5
1975 III	122.3	93.7	119.6	99.1	123.5
1975 IV	125.3	95.4	119.6	100.5	124.8
1976 I	127.5	98.1	119.8	102.7	124.1
1976 II	129.5	98.3	120.5	103.0	125.7
1976 III	130.3	96.6	121.9	101.9	127.9
1976 IV	129.8	96.5	121.9	101.8	127.4

Selected Bibliography

Abramovitz, M., and David, P.A. 1973. Reinterpreting economic growth: parables and realities. *American Economic Review* 63 (2).

Block, H. 1978. *The Planetary Product "Back to Normalcy" in 1976-1977.* Bureau of Intelligence and Research. Washington, D.C.: U.S. Department of State.

Boner, Barbara, and Neef, Arthur. 1977. Productivity and unit labor costs in 12 industrial countries. *Monthly Labor Review* 100 (7): 11-17.

Brown, Charles, and Medoff, James. 1978. Trade unions in the production process. *Journal of Political Economy* 86 (3): 355-78.

Bureau of Economic Analysis. 1977. *Gross National Product Data Improvement Project Report.* Report of the Advisory Committee on Gross National Product Data Improvement. Washington, D.C.: U.S. Department of Commerce.

Bureau of Labor Statistics. 1977. *Comparative Growth in Manufacturing Productivity and Labor Costs in Selected Industrialized Countries.* Bulletin 1958. Washington, D.C.: U.S. Department of Labor.

Christensen, L.R.; Cummings, D.; and Jorgenson, D.W. 1980. Economic growth, 1947-1973: an international comparison. In *New Developments in Productivity Measurement and Analysis*, John W. Kendrick and Beatrice N. Vaccara, eds. NBER Studies in Income and Wealth, vol. 44. Chicago: University of Chicago Press.

Clough, Anthony. 1970. *"Prices, Unit Labor Costs and Profits: An Examination of Wesley C. Mitchell's Business Cycle Theory for the Period 1947-1969."* Washington, D.C.: George Washington University, doctoral dissertation.

Davis, Hiram S. 1979. *Productivity Accounting.* Philadelphia: University of Pennsylvania Press.

Denison, Edward F. 1972. Classification of sources of growth. *Review of Income and Wealth* 18 (1): 1-25.

Denison, Edward F. 1974. *Accounting for U.S. Economic Growth, 1929-1969.* Washington, D.C.: Brookings Institution.

Denison, Edward F. 1978. Where has productivity gone? *Basis Point* 3 (1): 11-13. Published by the Equitable Life Insurance Association.

Denison, Edward F. 1978. Effects of selected changes in the institutional and human environment upon output per unit of input. *Survey of Current Business* (January).

Dutta, M. 1975. *Econometric Methods.* Cincinnati: Southwestern Publishing Co.

Fabricant, Solomon. 1968. Productivity. In *International Encyclopedia of the Social Sciences.* vol. 12, pp. 523-36. New York: Macmillan.

Gollop, F., and Jorgenson, D.W. 1980. U.S. Productivity growth by industry, 1947-1973. In *New Developments in Productivity Measurement and Analysis*, John W. Kendrick and Beatrice N. Vaccara, eds. NBER Studies in Income and Wealth, vol. 44. Chicago: University of Chicago Press.

Griliches, Zvi. 1980. Returns to research and development expenditures in the private sector. In *New Developments in Productivity Measurement and Analysis*, John W. Kendrick and Beatrice N. Vaccara, eds. NBER Studies in Income and Wealth, vol. 44. Chicago: University of Chicago Press.

Jorgenson, D.W., and Christensen, L. R. 1973. Measuring economic performance in the private sector. In *Measurement of Economic and Social Performance*, M. Moss, ed. Studies in Income and Wealth, vol. 38. New York: Columbia University Press.

Kendrick, John W. 1961. *Productivity Trends in the United States.* Princeton: Princeton University Press.

Kendrick, John W. 1973. *Postwar Productivity Trends in the United States, 1948-1969.* Prepared for the National Bureau of Economic Research. New York: Columbia University Press.

Kendrick, John W. 1976. *The Formation and Stocks of Total Capital.* New York: National Bureau of Economic Research.

Kendrick, John W. 1977. *Understanding Productivity: An Introduction to the Dynamics of Productivity Change.* Baltimore: The Johns Hopkins University Press.

Kendrick, John W. 1977. "Total Investment and Productivity Developments." Paper presented to the American Finance Association and the American Economic Association. New York, N.Y.

Kendrick, John W., and Creamer, Daniel. 1965. *Measuring Company Productivity: A Handbook with Case Studies.* New York: Conference Board, revised edition.

Kravis, Irving B. 1976. A survey of international comparisons of productivity. *Economic Journal* 86 (341) (March).

Kravis, Irving B.; Kennessey, Zoltan; Heston, Alan; and Summers, Robert. 1978. *International Comparisons of Real Product and Purchasing Power.* Report of the United Nations International Comparison Project: Phase Two. Baltimore: The Johns Hopkins University Press.

Kuznets, Simon. 1971. *Economic Growth of Nations: Total Output and Production Structure.* Cambridge, Mass.: Harvard University Press.

Leibenstein, Harvey. 1976. *Beyond Economic Man.* Cambridge, Mass.: Harvard University Press.

Mansfield, Edwin, et al. 1977. Social and private rates of return from industrial innovations. *Quarterly Journal of Economics* (May): 221-40.

Mitchell, Wesley C. 1913. *Business Cycles.* Berkeley: University of California Press.

Moore, Geoffrey. 1975. Productivity, costs and prices: new light from an old hypothesis. National Bureau of Economic Research, *Explorations in Economic Research* 2 (1) (Winter).

Myers, John G., et al. 1976. The impact of OPEC, FEA, EPA, and OSHA on productivity and growth. *The Conference Board Record* (April).

Myers, John G. 1977. The new realities in productivity and growth. *Business Economics* (January).

Nadiri, M. Ishaq. 1970. Some approaches to the theory and measurement of total factor productivity. *Journal of Economic Literature* (December).

National Center for Productivity and Quality of Working Life. 1976. *Improving Productivity through Industry and Company Measurement.* Washington, D.C.: National Center for Productivity and Quality of Working Life.

Norsworthy, J. R., and Harper, I. W. 1979. "The Role of Capital Formation in the Recent Productivity Slowdown." Bureau of Labor Statistics working paper no. 87. U.S. Department of Labor, Washington, D.C.

Solow, Robert M. 1957. Technical change and the aggregate production function. *Review of Economics and Statistics* 3 (August): 312-20.

Terleckyj, Nestor. 1974. *Effects of R&D on the Productivity Growth of Industries: An Exploratory Study.* Washington, D.C.: National Planning Association.

U.S. Department of Commerce, Bureau of Economic Analysis. 1972. The measurement of productivity. *Survey of Current Business* 52 (5), part 2.

U.S. Department of Commerce, Bureau of Economic Analysis. 1976. The national income and product accounts of the United States: revised estimates, 1929-74. *Survey of Current Business*, 56 (1). Publication of the Bureau of Economic Analysis.

U.S. Department of Commerce. *Business Conditions Digest.* Washington, D.C.: U.S. Government Printing Office, monthly.

U.S. President. 1979. *Economic Report of the President.* Washington, D.C.: U.S. Government Printing Office.

Index

Index

The Johns Hopkins University Press

This book was set by Culpeper Publishers in IBM Selectric Press Roman and printed on 50-lb. # 66 Eggshell Offset paper and bound by the Maple Press Company.

Library of Congress Cataloging in Publication Data

Kendrick, John W
    Productivity in the United States.

    Bibliography: pp. 161-63
    Includes index.
    1. Industrial productivity—United States.
I. Grossman, Elliot S., joint author. II. Title.
HC110.I52K46   338'.06   79-3678
ISBN 0-8018-2289-0